NIC STONE

Dear Martin

CORNELSEN
ENGLISH
LIBRARY

Cornelsen

CORNELSEN **ENGLISH** LIBRARY
Nic Stone: *Dear Martin*

Annotationen
Jana Lose, Benedikt Vogeler

Verlagsredaktion
Renata Jakovac (verantwortliche Redakteurin), Peadar Curran

Lizenzmanagement
Lena Goncharenko

Umschlaggestaltung
hawemannundmosch, Berlin

Titelbild
Stefan Bachmann, Wiesbaden

Layout & technische Umsetzung
Reemers, Berlin

Ebenfalls erhältlich:
Dear Martin Handreichungen für den Unterricht als Download 9783060360307

www.cornelsen.de

1. Auflage, 3. Druck 2024

Alle Drucke dieser Auflage sind inhaltlich unverändert und können
im Unterricht nebeneinander verwendet werden.

© 2023 Cornelsen Verlag GmbH, Berlin

Druck: H. Heenemann, Berlin

ISBN 978-3-060-36031-4

PEFC zertifiziert
Dieses Produkt stammt aus nachhaltig
bewirtschafteten Wäldern und kontrollierten
Quellen.

PEFC
PEFC/04-31-1156

www.pefc.de

Contents

Abbreviations and Annotations

abbr	abbreviation		i.e.	id est, that is
adj	adjective		infml	informal
AE	American English		n	noun
arch	archaic, outdated		pl	plural
BE	British English		sb.	somebody
derog	derogatory		sl	slang
e.g.	exempli gratia, for example		sth.	something
esp.	especially		usu.	usually
fig	figurative(ly)		v	verb
fml	formal			

The annotations are arranged chronologically; the first time a word is used is where you will find it explained.

To K and M.
Be your best.

&

To Mr. Casey Weeks.
Consider this my quietus.

I BELIEVE THAT UNARMED TRUTH AND
UNCONDITIONAL LOVE
WILL HAVE THE FINAL WORD IN REALITY.

—Reverend Dr. Martin Luther King Jr.
Nobel Peace Prize Acceptance Speech, December 10, 1964

PART ONE

CHAPTER 1

From where he's standing across the street, Justyce can see her: Melo Taylor, ex-girlfriend, slumped[1] over beside her Benz on the damp[2] concrete[3] of the FarmFresh parking lot. She's missing a shoe, and the contents of her purse are scattered around her like the guts
5 of a pulled party popper[4]. He knows she's stone drunk, but this is too much, even for her.

Jus shakes his head, remembering the judgment all over his best friend Manny's face as he left Manny's house not fifteen minutes ago.

10 The WALK symbol appears.

As he approaches, she opens her eyes, and he waves and pulls his earbuds out just in time to hear her say, "What the hell are you doing here?"

Justyce asks himself the same question as he watches her try—
15 and fail—to shift[5] to her knees. She falls over sideways and hits her face against the car door.

He drops down and reaches for her cheek—which is as red as the candy-apple[6] paint job[7]. "Damn, Melo, are you okay?"

She pushes his hand away. "What do you care?"

20 Stung[8], Justyce takes a deep breath. He cares a lot. Obviously. If he didn't, he wouldn't've[9] walked a mile from Manny's house at three in the morning (Manny's of the opinion that Melo's "the worst thing that ever happened" to Jus, so of course he refused[10] to give his boy a ride). All to keep his drunken disaster of an ex from driving.

25 He should walk away right now, Justyce should.

---

1 slumped over: fallen over **2** damp: slightly wet **3** concrete ['kɒŋkriːt]: *Beton*
4 party popper: *Konfettikanone* **5** shift (v): move **6** candy-apple: *kandierter*
Apfel **7** paint job (infml): the paint scheme of Melo's car **8** stung (adj): upset,
angry usu. by what sb. says/does **9** wouldn't've (infml): would not have
10 refuse to do sth.: say no to doing sth.

But he doesn't.

"Jessa called me," he tells her.

"That skank[1]—"

"Don't be like that, babe. She only called me because she cares about you."   5

Jessa had planned to take Melo home herself, but Mel threatened[2] to call the cops and say she'd been kidnapped if Jessa didn't drop her at her car.

Melo can be a little dramatic when she's drunk.

"I'm totally unfollowing her," she says (case in point). "In life *and*   10
online. Nosy[3] bitch."

Justyce shakes his head again. "I just came to make sure you get home okay." That's when it hits Justyce that while he might succeed in getting Melo home, he has no idea how he'll get back. He closes his eyes as Manny's words ring through his head: *This Captain Save-*   15
A-Ho[4] thing is gonna get you in trouble, dawg[5].

He looks Melo over. She's now sitting with her head leaned back against the car door, half-asleep, mouth open.

He sighs. Even drunk, Jus can't deny Melo's the finest girl he's ever laid eyes—not to mention *hands*—on.   20

She starts to tilt[6], and Justyce catches her by the shoulders to keep her from falling. She startles[7], looking at him wide-eyed, and Jus can see everything about her that initially caught his attention. Melo's dad is this Hall of Fame NFL linebacker (biiiiig black dude), but her mom is from Norway. She got Mrs. Taylor's milky Norwegian   25
complexion[8], wavy[9] hair the color of honey, and amazing green eyes that are kind of purple around the edge, but she has really full lips,

---

1 skank (sl, derog): offensive term of abuse usu. towards women **2** threaten to do sth. [ˈθretn]: (here) warn sb. that you will do sth. umpleasant if sb. does not do what you want **3** nosy: too interested in other people's affairs **4** ho (sl, derog): female prostitute, used as an offensive term to describe or insult a woman's character **5** dawg [dɔːg] (sl): close (male) friend, homie **6** tilt (v): move so that you risk falling over **7** startle (v): move slightly but suddenly, as if frightened or surprised **8** complexion [kəmˈplekʃn]: shade of skin color **9** wavy: having curves, not straight

a small waist[1], crazy curvy hips, and probably the nicest butt Jus has ever seen in his life.

That's part of his problem: he gets too tripped up by how beautiful she is. He never would've dreamed a girl as fine as her would
5 be into *him*.

Now he's got the urge to kiss her even though her eyes are red and her hair's a mess and she smells like vodka and cigarettes and weed[2]. But when he goes to push her hair out of her face, she shoves[3] his hand away again. "Don't touch me, Justyce."

10 She starts shifting her stuff around on the ground—lipstick, Kleenex, tampons, one of those circular thingies with the makeup in one half and a mirror in the other, a flask[4]. "Ugh, where are my keeeeeeeys?"

Justyce spots them in front of the back tire and snatches[5] them
15 up. "You're not driving, Melo."

"Give 'em[6]." She swipes[7] for the keys but falls into his arms instead. Justyce props[8] her against the car again and gathers[9] the rest of her stuff to put it back in her bag—which is large enough to hold a week's worth of groceries[10] (what is it with girls and purses
20 the size of duffel bags[11]?). He unlocks the car, tosses the bag on the floor of the backseat, and tries to get Melo up off the ground.

Then everything goes really wrong, really fast.

First, she throws up[12] all over the hoodie Jus is wearing.

Which belongs to Manny. Who specifically said, "Don't come
25 back here with throw-up on my hoodie."

Perfect.

Jus takes off the sweatshirt and tosses it in the backseat.

When he tries to pick Melo up again, she slaps him. Hard. "Leave me *alone*, Justyce," she says.

---

1 waist: body part above the hips **2** weed (infml): cannabis **3** shove away sb./sth. [ʃʌv]: push away sb./sth. **4** flask: bottle **5** snatch sb./sth. (v): grab sb./sth. **6** 'em (infml): them **7** swipe (v): move your arm and hand with a swinging motion to hit or grab **8** prop against: lean against **9** gather sth.: collect sth. **10** groceries ['grəʊsəri]: food and other goods sold at a supermarket **11** duffel bag (AE): large bag **12** throw up: *erbrechen*

"I can't do that, Mel. There's no way you'll make it home if you try to drive yourself."

He tries to lift her by the armpits and she spits in his face.

He considers walking away again. He could call her parents, stick her keys in his pocket, and bounce[1]. Oak Ridge is probably *the* safest neighborhood in Atlanta. She'd be fine for the twenty-five minutes it would take Mr. Taylor to get here.

But he can't. Despite Manny's assertion[2] that Melo needs to "suffer[3] some consequences for once," leaving her here all vulnerable[4] doesn't seem like the right thing to do. So he picks her up and tosses her over his shoulder.

Melo responds in her usual delicate[5] fashion: she screams and beats him on the back with her fists[6].

Justyce struggles[7] to get the back door open and is lowering her into the car when he hears the *WHOOOOP* of a short siren and sees the blue lights. In the few seconds it takes the police car to screech[8] to a stop behind him, Justyce settles Melo into the backseat.

Now she's gone catatonic[9].

Justyce can hear the approaching footsteps, but he stays focused on getting Melo strapped[10] in. He wants it to be *clear* to the cop that she wasn't gonna[11] drive so she won't be in even worse trouble.

Before he can get his head out of the car, he feels a tug[12] on his shirt and is yanked[13] backward. His head smacks the doorframe just before a hand clamps down on the back of his neck. His upper body slams onto the trunk[14] with so much force, he bites the inside of his cheek, and his mouth fills with blood.

---

1 bounce (v): (here) leave   **2** assertion [əˈsɜːrʃn]: a claim or opinion expressed by sb.   **3** suffer sth.: experience something unpleasant, such as injury, defeat or loss   **4** vulnerable [ˈvʌlnərəbl]: weak and easily hurt   **5** delicate [ˈdelɪkət]: careful, gentle (here used sarcastically)   **6** fist (n): hand with fingers tightly closed into the palm   **7** struggle to do sth. (v): have problems doing sth.   **8** screech (v): make a loud high unpleasant sound   **9** catatonic: not moving or responding   **10** strap sb./sth. in: *jmd./etwas anschnallen*   **11** gonna (infml): going to   **12** tug (n): hard pull   **13** yank (v): pull hard and fast   **14** trunk (AE): back of the car (where you put bags in)

Jus swallows, head spinning, unable to get his bearings[1]. The sting of cold metal around his wrists[2] pulls him back to reality.

Handcuffs.

It hits him: Melo's drunk beyond belief in the backseat of a car
5 she fully intended[3] to drive, yet *Jus* is the one in handcuffs.

The cop shoves him to the ground beside the police cruiser as he asks if Justyce understands his rights. Justyce doesn't remember hearing any rights, but his ears *had* been ringing from the two blows[4] to the head, so maybe he missed them. He swallows more blood.

10 "Officer, this is a big misundersta—" he starts to say, but he doesn't get to finish because the officer hits him in the face.

"Don't you say shit to me, you son of a bitch. I knew your punk ass was up to no good when I saw you walking down the road with that goddamn hood on."

15 So the hood was a bad idea. Earbuds too. Probably would've noticed he was being trailed[5] without them. "But, Officer, I—"

"You keep your mouth *shut*." The cop squats[6] and gets right in Justyce's face. "I know your kind: punks like you wander the streets of nice neighborhoods searching for prey[7]. Just couldn't resist the
20 pretty white girl who'd locked her keys in her car, could ya[8]?"

Except that doesn't even make sense. If Mel had locked the keys in the car, Jus wouldn't have been able to get her inside it, would he? Justyce finds the officer's nameplate; CASTILLO, it reads, though the guy looks like a regular white dude. Mama told him how to han-
25 dle this type of situation, though he must admit he never expected to actually need the advice: *Be respectful; keep the anger in check[9]; make sure the police can see your hands* (though that's impossible right now). "Officer Castillo, I mean you no disresp—"

"I told your punk ass to shut the fuck up!"

---

1 (get) one's bearings: knowledge of your position relative to everything that is
around or near you **2** wrist: body part between your hand and your arm
3 intend to: plan, have in mind **4** blow (n): hard strike **5** trail (v): follow
6 squat [skwɑːt] (v): sit on your heels **7** prey (n): victim **8** ya (infml): you
9 keep sth./sb. in check: keep sth./sb. under control

He wishes he could see Melo. Get her to tell this cop the truth. But the dude is blocking his view.

"Now, if you know what's good for you, you won't move or speak. Resistance[1] will only land you in deeper shit. Got it?"

Cigarette breath and flecks of spit hit Justyce's face as the cop speaks, but Justyce fixes his gaze[2] on the glowing green *F* of the FarmFresh sign.

"Look at me when I'm talking to you, boy." He grabs Justyce's chin. "I asked you a question."

Justyce swallows. Meets the cold blue of Officer Castillo's eyes. Clears his throat[3].

"Yes sir," he says. "I got it."

---

1 resistance: refusing to accept a situation by fighting back **2** gaze (n): intense look that is steady and fixed **3** clear one's throat: cough so that one can speak clearly

August 25

DEAR MARTIN (AKA DR. KING),

First and foremost[1], please know I mean you no disrespect with the whole "Martin" thing. I studied you and your teachings for a project in
5 tenth grade, so it feels most natural to interact with you as a homie. Hope you don't mind[2] that.

Quick intro: My name is Justyce McAllister. I'm a 17-year-old high school senior and full-scholarship[3] student at Braselton Preparatory Academy in Atlanta, Georgia.

10 I'm ranked fourth[4] in my graduating class of 83, I'm the captain of the debate team, I scored a 1560 and a 34 on my SATs[5] and ACTs respectively[6], and despite[7] growing up in a "bad" area (not too far from your old stomping grounds[8]), I have a future ahead of me that will likely include an Ivy League[9] education, an eventual law degree, and a career
15 in public policy[10].

Sadly, during the wee hours[11] of this morning, literally none of that mattered[12].

Long story short, I tried to do a good deed and wound up[13] on the ground in handcuffs. And despite the fact that my ex-girl was visibly
20 drunk off her ass, excuse my language, I apparently looked so menacing[14] in my prep school[15] hoodie, the cop who cuffed me called for backup.

The craziest part is while I thought everything would be cool as soon as her parents got there, no matter what they told the cops, these dudes would not release me.

---

1 first and foremost: most importantly **2** mind (v): be upset **3** scholarship ['skɑːlərʃɪp]: *Stipendium* **4** ranked fourth: fourth best **5** SATs/ACTs: test taken by high school students who want to go to college **6** respectively: *beziehungsweise* **7** despite: in spite of **8** stomping ground: a place that sb. likes and goes to very often **9** Ivy League [ˌaɪvi ˈliːg]: eight elite US universities **10** public policy: the field of government and law as it affects social affairs **11** wee hours: early hours **12** matter (v): be important **13** wind up: finish **14** menacing [ˈmenəsɪŋ]: dangerous **15** prep school: a school, usu. private, that prepares students for college

Mr. Taylor offered to call my mom, but the cops made it clear that since I'm 17, I'm considered an adult when placed under arrest—aka[1] there was nothing Mama could do.

Mr. Taylor wound up calling my friend SJ's mom, Mrs. Friedman— an attorney[2]—and she had to come bark[3] a bunch of legal hoo-ha[4] in   5 the cops' faces before they'd undo the cuffs. By the time they finally let me go, the sun was coming up.

It'd been hours, Martin.

Mrs. F didn't say a whole lot as she drove me to my dorm[5], but she made me promise to go by the infirmary[6] and get some cold packs for   10 my swollen wrists. I called my mama to tell her what happened, and she said she'll file a complaint[7] first thing in the morning. But I doubt[8] it'll do any good.

Frankly[9], I'm not real sure what to feel. Never thought I'd be in this kind of situation. There was this kid, Shemar Carson . . . black dude, my   15 age, shot and killed in Nevada by this white cop back in June. The details are hazy[10] since there weren't any witnesses[11], but what's clear is this cop shot an unarmed[12] kid. Four times. Even fishier[13], according to the medical examiners, there was a two-hour gap between the estimated[14] time of death and when the cop called it in.   20

Before The Incident last night, I hadn't really thought much about it. There's a lot of conflicting information, so it's hard to know what to believe. Shemar's family and friends say he was a good dude, headed[15] to college, active in his youth group . . . but the cop claims he caught She- mar trying to steal a car. A scuffle[16] ensued[17] (allegedly[18]), and according   25

---

1 aka [ˌeɪ keɪ ˈeɪ]: (here) in other words **2** attorney [əˈtɜːrni]: lawyer **3** bark (v): speak sharply, shout **4** legal hoo-ha: (here) legal language e.g. about human rights **5** dorm: a building for university or college students to live in **6** infir- mary [ɪnˈfɜːrməri]: medical facility in a school **7** file a complaint: send in a formal complaint **8** doubt (v) [daʊt]: not fully believe sth. **9** frankly: honestly **10** hazy: not clear **11** witness (n): person who sees sth. happen **12** unarmed: without weapons **13** fishy: seeming wrong **14** estimate (v): guess **15** head to: go in a certain direction **16** scuffle (n): fight **17** ensue [ɪnˈsuː]: happen after/as a result of another event **18** allegedly: said by sb. as a fact but not yet proved to be a fact

to the police report, Shemar tried to grab the cop's gun, so the cop shot Shemar in self-defense.

I dunno[1]. I've seen some pictures of Shemar Carson, and he did have kind of a thuggish[2] appearance. In a way, I guess I thought I didn't
5 really need to concern myself with this type of thing because compared to him, I don't come across as "threatening," you know? I don't sag my pants[3] or wear my clothes super big. I go to a good school, and have goals and vision and "a great head on my shoulders," as Mama likes to say.

10 Yeah, I grew up in a rough area, but I know I'm a good dude, Martin. I thought if I made sure to be an upstanding[4] member of society, I'd be exempt[5] from the stuff THOSE black guys deal with, you know? Really hard to swallow[6] that I was wrong.

All I can think now is "How different would things have gone had I
15 not been a black guy?" I know initially the cop could only go by what he saw (which prolly[7] did seem a little sketchy[8]), but I've never had my character challenged like that before.

Last night changed me. I don't wanna[9] walk around all pissed off[10] and looking for problems, but I know I can't continue to pretend noth-
20 ing's wrong. Yeah, there are no more "colored[11]" water fountains, and it's supposed to be illegal to discriminate, but if I can be forced to sit on the concrete in too-tight[12] cuffs when I've done nothing wrong, it's clear there's an issue. That things aren't as equal as folks[13] say they are.

I need to pay more attention, Martin. Start really seeing stuff and
25 writing it down. Figure out what to do with it. That's why I'm writing to you. You faced way worse shi[14]—I mean stuff than sitting in handcuffs

---

1 dunno (infml): don't know **2** thuggish: violent **3** sag my pants (infml): wear baggy jeans loose so that underwear is visible **4** upstanding: *aufrecht*
5 exempt from sth.: (here) free from sth., not affected by sth. **6** hard to swallow: hard to accept/believe **7** prolly (infml): probably **8** sketchy (AE, infml): (here) bad **9** wanna (infml): want to **10** pissed off (infml): angry **11** colored: used to describe non-white people during the era of segregation, now considered offensive **12** tight (adj): fitting closely **13** folks: people **14** shi- (infml): shit

for a few hours, but you stuck to your guns[1] . . . Well, your lack thereof[2], actually.

I wanna try to live like you. Do what you would do. See where it gets me.

My wrist is killing me, so I have to stop writing now, but thanks for ⁵ hearing me out[3].

Sincerely,
Justyce McAllister

---

1 stick to your guns: continue your action or keep your belief in sth. despite other people disagreeing with you **2** your lack thereof: not having sth. which has just been spoken about (here: guns); (here) meaning Martin Luther King Jr. did not want or have guns **3** hear sb. out: allow sb. to speak until they've said all they have to say and not interrupt

CHAPTER 2

Justyce drops down onto the plush leather sofa in Manny's basement and grabs the game controller from the giant ottoman[1] in
front of him.

"You good, dawg?" Manny says, furiously[2] pressing buttons on
5 his vibrating controller as the sound of machinegun fire fills the
room in surround sound. It pushes into Justyce's ears and bounces[3]
around in his head; he can feel it pulsating[4] in his chest: *BANG-
BANGBANGBANGBANGBANGBANG-BANGBANGBANGBANG.*

He gulps[5]. "Yeah. I'm good."

10 "So you playing, or what?"

Manny's avatar switches[6] weapons in quick succession[7], tossing
everything he's got at the enemy troops.

Grenade[8]: *BOOM.*

Glock[9] 26: *POP POP POP.*

15 Flamethrower[10]: *FWHOOSH.*

Bazooka[11]: *FWUUUUMP . . . BOOOOOOM.*

So many guns. Just like the one Castillo kept his hand on while
treating[12] Jus like a criminal. One wrong move, and Jus might've been
the next Shemar Carson.

20 He shudders[13]. "Hey, you mind if we play something a little less
. . . violent?"

---

1 ottoman: low seat **2** furiously: (here) with great speed and energy **3** bounce
(v): jump **4** pulsate ['pʌlseɪt]: make strong regular movements **5** gulp (v):
swallow, but without eating or drinking, because of fear or surprise **6** switch (v):
change **7** succession: one after another **8** grenade: *Granate* **9** Glock: type of
pistol **10** flamethrower: *Flammenwerfer* **11** bazooka: common name of
man-portable antitank rocket launcher during WW II **12** treat sb. (v): behave
towards sb. **13** shudder (v): shake with fear

Manny pauses the game. Turns to his best friend. "Sorry." Justyce drops his head. "Can't really handle[1] the gunshots and stuff right now."

Manny reaches out to give Jus's shoulder a supportive[2] squeeze[3], then pushes a few buttons to switch games. The new Madden[4]. Which doesn't even hit the shelves[5] for another week.

Justyce shakes his head. If only he had his best friend's life. Must be nice having the VP[6] of a major financial corporation[7] for a dad.

The guys choose their respective teams. Manny wins the coin toss and elects to receive[8]. He clears his throat. "You wanna talk about it?"

Justyce sighs.

"You know I'm like . . . *here* if you do, right?" Manny says.

"Yeah, I know, Manny. I appreciate[9] it. Just not real sure what to say."

Manny nods. Puts a spin move[10] on Justyce's defensive lineman[11] and gets the first down. "Wrists feelin' any better?"

Justyce fights the urge[12] to look at his arms. It's hard to see the bruises because his skin is such a deep brown, but even after a week, they're still there.

Sometimes he thinks they'll never fade[13].

"Yeah, they're all right. Mel gave me this weird ointment[14] from Norway. Smells like Altoid-covered[15] feet, but it's doing the trick." Manny's quarterback throws a deep pass, but it's short. Justyce's free safety[16] intercepts[17]. "We got back together last night."

Manny presses Pause. Turns to his boy.

---

1 handle (v): deal or cope with **2** supportive: encouraging sb. by showing sympathy **3** squeeze (n): press with fingers **4** Madden (NFL): American football video game **5** hit the shelves: be on sale in shops **6** VP: vice president **7** corporation: company **8** receive: (here) the attacking team in American football **9** appreciate sb./sth. [əˈpriːʃɪeɪt]: value what sb. does for you **10** put a spin move on sb./sth.: turn sb./sth. around **11** defensive lineman: player who prevents the other team from scoring **12** urge [ɜːdʒ] (n): strong desire or impulse to do sth. **13** fade: lose colour/become less visible **14** ointment: cream **15** Altoid: mint sweets for fresh breath **16** safety: (here) defensive player **17** intercept: stop sb./sth.

"Dawg, you are *not* serious right now."

Justyce reaches over and hits the triangle button on Manny's controller. Jus's QB[1] tosses the ball to his running back—who is unguarded since Manny's stare is burning a hole in the side of Jus's face. The virtual player runs it in for the easy touchdown.

The kick is good.

Manny pauses again. "Jus."

"Let it go, man."

"Let it *go*? That ho is the reason you sat in handcuffs for *three hours,* and you want me to let it *go*?"

"Stop callin' my girl a ho, Manny."

"Bro, you caught this girl wrist-deep in another dude's pants. Helloooo?"

"It's different this time." Justyce starts the game again.

His team kicks off, but Manny's players don't move because he's still gaping[2] at Justyce like he just confessed[3] to murder. "Hold up[4]," Manny says, stopping the game and tossing his controller out of Jus's reach[5]. "So you mean to tell me that after this girl sat there and *watched* this cop brutalize your ass—"

"She was scared, man."

"Unbelievable, Jus."

"Whatever." Justyce stares at the football frozen in midair on the massive flat-screen. Girls don't flock[6] to Justyce like they do to Emmanuel "Manny" Rivers, Bras Prep[7] basketball captain and one of the best-looking guys Jus knows. There's a lot of stuff Manny has that Justyce doesn't—two parents with six-figure salaries[8], a basement apartment, a badass[9] car, crazy confidence[10] . . .

What does Justyce have? The hottest girl in school.

---

1 QB: quarterback, players' position on offense and defense in American football
2 gape (v): stare in surprise at sb./sth. **3** confess to: admit to **4** hold up: stop
5 reach (n): distance you can stretch your arm over to touch sth. **6** flock (v): come together in large numbers **7** Bras Prep: name of high school **8** six-figure salary: when you get paid $100,000 or more for your work **9** badass: very cool
10 confidence: belief in yourself

"I don't expect you to understand, Manny. You run through girls like underwear. Wouldn't know true love if it kicked you in the nuts."

"First of all, true love *wouldn't* kick me in the nuts. Considering[1] how many times Melo has figuratively[2] kicked you in yours—"

"Shut up, man."   5

Manny shakes his head. "I hate to break[3] it to you, homie, but you and Melo's relationship puts the *ick* in *toxic*[4]."

"That's some girly shit you just said, dawg."

"You know my mom's a psychologist," Manny says. "You got Codependency[5] Syndrome or something. You should really take a   10
look at that."

"Thanks, Dr. Phil[6]."

"I'm serious, Jus. I can't even look at you right now. This thing you're doing? This always-running-back-to-Melo thing? It's a sickness, my friend."   15

"Shut up and play the damn game, man."

Just then Manny's mom appears at the foot of the stairs.

"Hi, Dr. Rivers," Justyce says, rising to give her a hug.

"Hey, baby. You doin' all right?"

"Yes ma'am."   20

"You sleeping over[7]? Dinner will be ready in a few. Chicken cacciatore[8]." She winks[9].

"Aww, you know that's my favorite," Jus says.

"Dang, Ma, how come you don't never make *my* favorite?"

"Don't *ever*, Emmanuel. And hush[10]."   25

"Don't be mad cuz your mom likes me more than you, Manny."

"Shut up, fool[11]."

---

1 consider: think about **2** figuratively: not literally **3** break sth. to sb. (v): (here) tell bad news to sb. **4** toxic: poisonous, harmful **5** codependency [ˌkəʊdɪˈpendənsi]: a relationship where both people need each other too much, esp. when one is caring for another due to illness or addiction **6** Dr. Phil: famous American doctor who gives advice on TV **7** sleep over: stay overnight **8** Chicken cacciatore [ˌkɑːtʃəˈtɔːri]: spicy Italian chicken meal prepared with tomatoes, mushrooms, herbs, and other seasonings **9** wink (v): *zwinkern* **10** hush (v): be quiet **11** fool (n): idiot

Dr. Rivers's cell phone rings. "This is Tiffany Rivers," she says when she answers, still smiling at the boys.

Doesn't last long. Whoever's on the other end of the phone, it's obvious from her expression[1] they're not bearing[2] good news.

5   She hangs up and puts her hand over her heart.

"Mom? Everything okay?"

"That was your aunt," she says. "Your cousin's been arrested."

Manny rolls his eyes. "What'd he do this time?"

Dr. Rivers looks from Manny to Justyce and back again. "He's 10 been charged[3] with murder," she says.

Manny's jaw[4] drops.

"They say he killed a police officer."

---

1 expression: way sb. looks **2** bear sth.: bring sth. **3** charged with: officially accused of a crime **4** jaw [dʒɔː]: bone that forms the lower part of the mouth

CHAPTER 3

Justyce has a lot on his mind as he steps into his Societal Evolution[1] class on Tuesday. For one, yesterday a Nevada grand jury[2] didn't return an indictment[3] on the cop who killed Shemar Carson. Since being arrested, Justyce has spent all his free time following the case, and now it's just . . . over. 5

Speaking of cops and arrests, yesterday Justyce also learned that the cop Manny's cousin confessed to shooting was none other[4] than Tomás Castillo.

What Jus can't get over is that he *knows* Manny's cousin. His name is Quan Banks, and he lives in Justyce's mom's neighborhood. 10 Quan's a year younger than Justyce, and they played together back when the only thing that mattered was staying outside until the streetlights came on. Like Justyce, Quan tested into the Accelerated Learners[5] program in third grade, but when elementary school ended, Quan started running with[6] a not-so-great crowd[7]. 15

When Quan found out Justyce was headed to Bras Prep, he mentioned[8] a cousin who went there, but Jus never put two and two together[9]. And now Quan's in jail.

Justyce can't stop thinking about it.

---

1 Societal Evolution: school subject about societal and cultural change over time **2** grand jury: a jury that has to decide whether there is enough evidence (*Beweise*) against an accused person for a trial in court **3** return an indictment [ɪnˈdaɪtmənt]: decide there is enough evidence to put a person on trial for a crime **4** none other: that very person or thing **5** Accelerated [əkˈsɛləˌreɪtɪd] Learners program: program that allows students to go through their education faster **6** run with sb. (AE): *sich mit jmd. herumtreiben* **7** crowd (n): *(hier) Clique, Gruppe von Menschen* **8** mention (v): speak of **9** put two and two together: conclude from obvious evidence

Yeah, Castillo was an asshole, but did he really deserve[1] to die? And what about Quan? What if they give him the death penalty?

What if Castillo had killed Jus, though? Would he have even been indicted[2]?

5   "Come here for a second, Jus," Doc says as Justyce drops his backpack on the floor beside his seat. Dr. Jarius "Doc" Dray is the debate team advisor[3] and Justyce's favorite teacher at Bras Prep. He's the only (half) black guy Jus knows with a PhD[4], and Jus really looks up to him. "How you holding up, my man?" Doc says.

10   "Been better, Doc."

Doc nods and narrows[5] his green eyes. "Figured as much," he says. "I wanted to let you know today's discussion might hit a nerve. Feel free to sit it out[6]. You can leave the room if need be[7]."

"All right."

15   Just then, Manny comes into the room with Jared Christensen at his heels[8]. Justyce isn't real fond[9] of Jared—or any of Manny's other friends for that matter—but he knows they've all been tight[10] since kindergarten, so he tries to keep a lid on it[11].

"What's up, Doc?" Jared crows[12] as he crosses the room to his
20 seat.

"Oh god, Jared. Sit *down* somewhere." That would be Sarah-Jane Friedman. Lacrosse[13] captain, future valedictorian[14], and Justyce's debate partner since sophomore[15] year.

"Aww[16], SJ, I love you too," Jared says.

---

1 deserve sth.: get sth., e.g. a reward or punishment, because of your actions or qualities **2** indict [ɪnˈdaɪt]: (officially) accuse **3** advisor: instructor **4** PhD: *Doktortitel* **5** narrow sth. (v): make sth. less wide **6** sit sth. out: not take part in sth. **7** if need be: if necessary **8** at sb.'s heels: closely behind sb. **9** be fond of sb./sth.: really like sb./sth. **10** tight: (here) close friends **11** keep a lid on sth.: keep sth. secret **12** crow (v): say sth. happily **13** lacrosse [ləˈkrɔːs]: outdoor game **14** valedictorian [ˌvælɪdɪkˈtɔːriən]: student with the highest grades **15** sophomore [ˈsɑːfəmɔːr]: student in the second year of college/university **16** aww [ɔː]: sound used to show your appreciation of sth. nice

SJ glares[1] at him and pretends to shove a finger down her throat[2] as she approaches the seat to Justyce's left. It makes him laugh.

The rest of the class trickles[3] in, and the moment the bell rings, Doc pushes the door shut and claps his hands to begin class: 5

Doc: Morning, peeps.

Class: [*Multiple grunts[4], waves, and nods.*]

Doc: Let's get started, shall we? Discussion prompt[5] of the day . . .

[*He makes a few taps on his laptop, and the words* all men are created equal[6] *appear*[7] *on the classroom's digital chalkboard[8].*]   10

Doc: Who can tell me the origin of this statement?

Jared: United States Declaration of Independence[9], ratified[10] July Fourth, 1776. [*Smiles smugly[11] and crosses his arms.*]

Doc: Correct, Mr. Christensen. Twelve of the thirteen colonies voted in favor[12] of severing[13] all ties[14] to the British throne. The document known   15 as the Declaration of Independence was written into being, and to this day, one of the most oft-quoted[15] lines of said[16] document is what you see there on the board.

Everyone: [*Nods.*]

---

1 glare at sb./sth.: look at sb./sth. in an angry way **2** shove a finger down your throat: put your finger far into your mouth to make yourself vomit **3** trickle in (v): come in slowly **4** grunt (n): low pig-like sound **5** prompt (n): (here) short phrase used to inspire a debate/ideas/etc. **6** "All men are created equal": phrase from the United States Declaration of Independence of 1776 **7** appear: come into sight **8** chalkboard (AE): blackboard **9** Declaration of Independence: document from 1776 that states that the thirteen British colonies in America are independent from Britain **10** ratify sth.: make sth. official by signing it or voting for it **11** smugly: in a way that shows you feel too pleased about something you have done or achieved **12** in favor of sth.: in support of sth., agree with sth. **13** severe sth. ['sevər]: cut sth. completely off **14** tie (n): connection **15** oft-quoted: *viel zitiert* **16** said (adj): mentioned before

Doc: Now, when we use our twenty-first-century minds to examine the quote within its historical context, something about it isn't quite right. Can anyone explain what I mean?

Everyone: [*Crickets*[1].]

5 Doc: Oh, come on, y'all[2]. You don't see anything odd[3] about *these* guys in particular making a statement about the inherent[4] "equality" of men?

SJ: Well, these were the same guys who killed off the indigenous[5] peoples and owned slaves.

Doc: Indeed they were.

10 Jared: But it was different then. Neither[6] slaves nor Indians—

Justyce: Native Americans or American Indians if you can't name the tribe, homie.

Jared: Whatever. Point is, neither were really considered "men."

Doc: That's exactly my point, Mr. Christensen. So here's the question: What
15 does the obvious[7] change in the application[8] of this phrase from 1776 to now tell us about how our society has evolved[9]?

[*Extended*[10] *pause as he adds the question to the digital chalkboard beneath*[11] *the quote, then the scrape*[12] *of a chair as he takes his regular seat in the circle.*]

Jared: Well, for one, people of African descent[13] are obviously included in
20 the application of the quote now. So are *"Native American Indians."*

Justyce: [*Clenches*[14] *jaw.*]

---

1 crickets ['krɪkɪt] (n, infml): no reaction at all; *Grillen* 2 y'all (infml): you all
3 odd: unusual 4 inherent [ɪn'herənt]: a natural part of sb. or sth. 5 indigenous
[ɪn'dɪdʒənəs]: native 6 neither... nor...: sth. that is not true for two things
7 obvious ['ɑːbviəs]: clear 8 application: (here) use 9 evolve: develop
10 extended: (here) long 11 beneath [bɪ'niːθ]: below 12 scrape (n): sound of
two things unpleasantly rubbing against each other 13 descent [dɪ'sent]: social/
national background 14 clench sth.: press sth. together tightly

Jared: And women! Women were originally excluded, but now things are more equal for them too.

SJ: [*Snorts[1].*] Still not equal enough.

Doc: Expound[2] if you will, Ms. Friedman.

SJ: It's simple: women still aren't treated as men's equals. Especially by men. 5

Jared: [*Rolls eyes.*]

Doc: Okay. So there's Women's Rights. Any other areas where you guys feel like we haven't quite reached the equality bar[3]?

Everyone: [...]

Doc: Feel free to consider current[4] events. 10

SJ: You would make a terrible lawyer, Doc.

Everyone: [*Nervous laughter.*]

Doc: I *know* y'all know what I'm getting at[5] here.

Manny: I mean, we do But you really wanna go there, Doc?

Doc: Hey, this school prides[6] itself on open dialogue. So let's hear it. 15

Everyone: [...]

Doc: I'll come right out[7] with it, then: Do you guys feel we've achieved full "equality" with regard[8] to race?

Everyone: [...]

Doc: Come on, guys. This is a safe space. Nothing said here today leaves 20 this room.

---

1 snort (v): make a sound by breathing through your nose **2** expound sth. to sb.: explain sth. in detail **3** equality bar: level of equality **4** current (adj): happening now **5** get at sth.: (here) hint at sth. **6** pride yourself on doing sth. (v): be proud of sth. **7** come right out with sth.: clearly say sth. **8** with regard to sb./sth.: relating to sb./sth.

Jared: Okay, I'll bite[1]. In my opinion, yes: we *have* reached full equality when it comes to race.

Doc: Expound, please.

Jared: Well, anyone born here is a citizen with full rights. There are people
5 who claim[2] certain "injustices" are race-related, but if you ask me, they're just being divisive[3].

Justyce: [*Inhales[4] deeply and rubs[5] his wrists.*]

Jared: America's a pretty color-blind[6] place now.

SJ: Of course *you* would say that.

10 Manny: Oh boy.

SJ: It never ceases[7] to amaze me that guys like you have your heads so far up your entitled[8] asses—

Doc: Sarah-Jane.

SJ: Sorry. It's just—you're completely oblivious[9] to the struggles of anyone
15 outside your little social group.

Jared: Whatever, SJ.

SJ: I'm serious. What about the economic disparities[10]? What about the fact that proportionally[11] speaking, there are more people of color living in poverty than white people? Have you even *thought* about that?

20 Jared: Dude, Manny drives a Range Rover.

Manny: What does that have to do with anything?

---

1 bite (v): (here) react to a provocative statement **2** claim sth.: say sth. is true **3** divisive [dɪˈvaɪsɪv] (adj): causing people to argue and separate **4** inhale: breathe in **5** rub: massage sth. with your fingers **6** color-blind: treating people of different skin colours the same **7** cease [siːs]: stop **8** entitled (adj.): privileged, honored **9** oblivious [əˈblɪviəs]: ignorant, not aware of sth. **10** disparities: differences/inequality between social groups which can be financial, racial, educational, etc. **11** proportional: in comparison

Jared: No beef[1], dude. I'm just saying your folks make way more money than mine.

Manny: Okay. They worked really hard to get to where they are, so—

Jared: I'm not saying they didn't, dude. You just proved my point. Black people have the same opportunities as white people in this country if they're   5
willing to work hard enough. Manny's parents are a perfect example.

SJ: Seriously? You really think one example proves things are equal? What about Justyce? His mom works sixty hours a week, but she doesn't make a *tenth* of what your dad ma—

Justyce: S, chill with that, man.   10

SJ: Sorry, Jus. What I'm saying is Manny's parents are an exception[2]. Have you not noticed there are only eight black kids in our whole school?

Jared: Well, maybe if more people were like Manny's parents, that wouldn't be the case.

Justyce: [*Takes another deep breath.*]   15

SJ: Ah, okay . . . so you're saying people just need to pull themselves up by their bootstraps[3]?

Jared: Exactly.

SJ: In order to do that, they have to be able to afford[4] boots.

Manny: Dang[5]. Point for SJ.   20

Jared: Whatever. There are people on welfare[6] strutting[7] around in Air Jordans, so there's obviously some footwear money coming from somewhere.

---

1 no beef (infml): no trouble 2 exception: sth. that does not follow the general rule 3 pull yourself up by your bootstraps: improve your situation without help from others 4 afford sth.: have enough money to pay for sth. 5 dang (infml): damn 6 welfare: financial help for poor people 7 strut (v): walk in a proud way

And don't get all high and mighty[1], SJ. Your ancestors[2] owned slaves just like mine did.

SJ: Wrong, numbnuts[3]—

Doc: Ms. Friedman . . .

5 SJ: Sorry, Doc. As I was saying, *my* great-grandparents immigrated to this country from Poland after narrowly[4] escaping Chelmno.

Jared: *What?*

SJ: It was a Nazi death camp[5]. And you just proved my point again. You'd spew[6] a lot less asininity[7] if you were willing to see beyond[8] the eighteenth
10 hole of your country club golf course.

Doc: Reel[9] it in, SJ.

Jared: Just so you know, Manny's parents have been members of our country club longer than we have.

Manny: Bro!

15 Jared: Just sayin', dude.

SJ: God. This country is headed to hell in a handbasket with people like you at the helm[10], Jared.

Justyce: [*Chuckles[11].*]

---

1 high and mighty: behavior showing you think you are better than others
2 ancestor ['ænsestər]: family member that lived a long time ago **3** numbnut
['nʌm‚nʌt]: stupid person **4** narrowly: just, closely **5** Nazi death camp: one of many locations where the planned genocide of Jewish people and other groups was carried out by Germany in WWII **6** spew [spju:]: throw up **7** asininity
[‚æsə'nɪnəti] (AE): stupidity **8** beyond: further, more than sth. **9** reel sth. in:
(here) take sth. back **10** at the helm: in control **11** chuckle ['tʃʌkl] (v): laugh quietly

Jared: Anyway, to those unfamiliar[1] with the US Constitution[2], thanks to the Fourteenth Amendment[3], every person in this country has the right to life, liberty, and the pursuit of happiness—

SJ: Bullshit.

Doc: SJ!   5

SJ: It's true!

Justyce: You need to chill, S.

SJ: Are you serious?

Justyce: Yeah, I am.

SJ: You of all people know I'm right, Jus—   10

Justyce: Leave me outta[4] this.

SJ: Fine. Bottom line[5], it's been over two centuries[6], and African Americans are still getting a raw deal[7].

Jared: Coulda fooled me[8].

SJ: Oh my god. Do you watch the news at all[9]? The name Shemar Carson 15
ring a bell, maybe?

Jared: Ah, here we go. Not every white person who kills a black person is guilty of a crime. Pretty sure the courts proved that yesterday.

SJ: All the courts "proved" yesterday was that a white guy can kill an unarmed teenager and get away[10] with it if the kid is black.   20

---

1 unfamiliar with: not having any knowledge or experience of something
2 US Constitution: US system of laws **3** Fourteenth Amendment: a section added to the US Constitution in 1866 that gave all Americans equal rights and allowed former slaves to become citizens **4** outta (infml): out of **5** bottom line: the most important thing that you have to consider or accept; the essential point in a discussion **6** century: one hundred years **7** get a raw deal: receiving unfair treatment **8** Coulda fooled me: You could have fooled me. = I don't believe what you say. **9** at all: ever **10** get away with sth.: not punished for sth., e.g. a crime

Doc: Conjecture, SJ. You know better. You two need to tread[1] carefully here.

Jared: Dude, the kid attacked the cop and tried to take his gun.

And he had a criminal record[2].

Justyce: Hold up, man. The attack was *alleged.* There weren't any witnesses—

5   Jared: I thought you were staying out of it?

Doc: Watch it, Mr. Christensen.

Jared: He said it, not me.

Justyce: [*Grits[3] teeth.*]

SJ: Maybe if you actually followed the case instead of getting your informa-
10   tion from social media—

Jared: Doesn't change the fact that the guy'd been arrested before. You don't get arrested if you're not doing anything wrong. Bottom line, he was a criminal.

SJ: The charge on his record—which is public, so you can go look it up—was
15   a misdemeanor[4] possession[5] of marijuana.

Jared: So? Do the crime, do the time.

SJ: Jared, you bought an ounce[6] of weed two days ago—

Doc: Don't make me write you up[7] , SJ.

SJ: I saw it with my own eyes, Doc!

20   Jared: What I do with my money is none of your or anyone else's business[8].

---

1 tread (v): walk **2** criminal record: a history of being found guilty of crime(s) in the past **3** grit your teeth: bite your teeth together **4** misdemeanor [ˌmɪs-dɪˈmiːnər] (fml): not very bad crime **5** possession: something that you own or have with you at a particular time **6** ounce: unit of weight; 28,35 gr **7** write sb. up: (here) give sb. a formal written warning about their behaviour **8** be none of your business (infml): It is private and of no interest to you

Justyce: [*Snorts.*] Course[1] it's not. But what Shemar did with his is every-one's, right?

Doc: Y'all better get back on topic before I start handing out detentions[2].

SJ: My point is I've *seen* you commit[3] the same crime Shemar Carson had on   5
the "criminal record" you mentioned.

Jared: Whatever, SJ.

SJ: I know you'd prefer to ignore this stuff because you benefit[4] from it, but walking around pretending inequality doesn't exist won't make it disap-pear[5], Jared. You and Manny, who are equal in pretty much every way apart from race, could commit the same crime, but it's almost guaranteed that he   10
would receive a harsher[6] punishment than you.

Manny: Why do I keep getting pulled[7] into this?

Jared: Obviously because you're black, bro.

Everyone: [*Snickers*[8].]

SJ: Numbers don't lie.   15

Justyce: [*Rubs his wrists again.*]

Jared: Yeah, yeah. We get it. Your mom's the big-shot[9] attorney. You have *alllllll* the facts.

SJ: Deflect[10] all you want, but you can't deny[11] that you get away with stuff Manny could never get away with.   20

Manny: I swear I'm changing my name.

Jared: Maybe I get away with it because I'm not dumb enough to get caught.

Justyce: Wow.

---

1 course (infml): of course **2** detention: *Nachsitzen* **3** commit sth.: do sth., usu. a crime or sin **4** benefit (v): get sth. good out of sth. **5** disappear: go away
6 harsh: rough **7** pull into: (here) include **8** snicker (v): laugh quietly
9 big shot: important person **10** deflect: not accept criticism **11** deny: say that sth. is wrong

SJ: You get away with it because you're white, asshole.

Doc: Sarah-Jaaaaaaane—

Jared: You looked in a mirror lately, SJ? You're just as white as I am.

SJ: Yeah, and I recognize that and how it benefits me.

5 Jared: Do you? Sounds like you're jumping on the White Is Wrong bandwagon[1] to me.

Justyce: [*Cracks[2] his knuckles and shakes his head.*]

SJ: Whatever, Jared. Bottom line, nobody sees *us* and automatically assumes[3] we're up to no good.

10 Everyone: [. . .]

SJ: We'll never be seen as criminals before we're seen as people.

Everyone: [. . .]

Justyce: I'm going to the bathroom. [*Gets up and leaves.*]

---

1 jump on the bandwagon: join a side that is popular or likely to be successful
2 crack your knuckles: (here) flex your hands **3** assume: guess that sth. is true without knowing exactly

CHAPTER 4

Due to[1] the restaurant-like setup of the Bras Prep senior lounge, Jared, Manny, and their "crew"—Kyle Berkeley, Tyler Clepp, and Blake Benson—don't see Justyce sitting in the back booth[2] when they come in.

True to form[3], Jared disregards[4] Doc's "everything stays in this room" directive, and since he's obviously under the impression[5] that he and his bros have the lounge to themselves, he doesn't bother[6] to keep his voice down once the five of them are seated:

Jared: Can you believe that asshole? What kind of teacher has the nerve to suggest there's racial inequality to a classroom full of millennials[7]?

Kyle: Seriously, bro? He said that shit?

Jared: I kid[8] you not, bro. The dean[9] should fire his ass. I seriously might have my dad give the school a call.

Tyler: Damn, homie.

Jared: And of course SJ jumped right on it. I think the fact that her mom has to constantly[10] defend[11] all those thugs[12] is starting to screw[13] with her head.

Blake, Kyle, and Tyler: [*Laugh.*]

---

1 due to: because of 2 booth: small area separated from the public 3 true to form: in the expected, typical way 4 disregard: ignore 5 be under the impression that: believe sth. is true 6 not bother: not do or use sth. because it seems unnecessary 7 millennials: people born between 1980 and the late 1990s 8 kid sb. (v): tell sb. sth. untrue, as a joke 9 dean: an authority at university 10 constantly: all the time 11 defend sb.: (here) represent sb. in court 12 thug: violent, criminal person 13 screw with sb.'s head: (here) drive sb. crazy

Manny: [*Laughs belatedly[1].*]

Jared: If you ask me, she wants Justyce to pop her little cherry[2].

Kyle: Well, seeing as *you* never did it . . .

Jared: Shut up. We were in eighth grade.

5 Blake: You still totally wanna tap that, bro.

Kyle: Too late, though . . . if Justyce is your competition, you're screwed, dog. "Once you go black," right, Manny?

Manny: [*Snorts.*]

Tyler: Too bad for SJ, Justyce has his hands full with Melo Taylor—literally.

10 Jared: Which makes no sense to me, bro. What the hell does a hottie like Melo Taylor see in a guy who can't afford a Happy Meal?

Manny: Maybe it's not about money, J.

Jared: Says the dude who drives a Range Rover.

Blake, Kyle, and Tyler: [*Laugh.*]

15 Manny: Dawg, what *is* it with you today?

Jared: I'm just sick of people suggesting[3] African Americans still have it *so hard* these days. I don't care what SJ says, Manny. Your parents are totally proof[4] that things are equal now.

Blake: They really are.

---

1 belated: late 2 pop a woman's cherry (sl): *eine Frau entjungfern*; offensive expression for taking a woman's virginity, it implies taking it as a trophy
3 suggest [səˈdʒest]: propose an idea or plan 4 proof: fact that shows that sth. is definitely true

Jared: Right here, right now, on these red hills of Georgia, a son of former slaves and sons of former slave owners are sitting down at the table of brotherhood[1], dude. The Dream has been realized!

Tyler: Damn, bro. That was really poetic.

Manny: That's from the I Have a Dream speech[2], T.   5

Jared: Remember, bro? I had to memorize[3] that shit for our eighth-grade Heritage[4] Play.

Blake: That's right! Token[5] black guy over here got sick or something, right?

Jared: Exactly.

Kyle: You had *one* job, Manny.   10

Manny: Shut up, fool.

Jared: I still remember the whole speech.

Manny: That wasn't the whole speech, J.

Jared: Whatever. It was the most important part, and I remember all of it. They put brown makeup on me and everything.   15

Blake: I remember that, dude! You totally got a standing ovation[6]!

Kyle: See, things really are equal nowadays, bro. A white kid can play a famous black dude in a play, and it's no big deal.

---

1 table of brotherhood: reference to Martin Luther King's "I have a dream" speech – in which he hopes that one day Black and white people will sit together like brothers **2** I Have a Dream (speech): speech on racial equality given by Dr. Martin Luther King Jr. at the Washington memorial on 28/08/1963
3 memorize: learn word-for-word **4** heritage ['herɪtɪdʒ]: tradition, background
5 token (Black person, blind person, etc.): a single person from a minority group included in a company board, team, TV show, play, etc. in an attempt to appear diverse **6** standing ovation: people standing up from their seats for applause

Jared: Exactly! This is a color-blind society, my brethren[1] . . . people are judged by the content[2] of their character instead of the color of their skin.

Kyle: Right, dude. Like I totally don't even see you as black, Manny!

[*Manny laughs at this, but Justyce can tell his heart isn't in it. The statement*
5 *makes Justyce think about those handcuffs . . . these fools might not "see"*
Manny "as black," but Justyce knows damn well the police would.]

Jared: My brothers, let us raise our Perrier[3] bottles to EQUALITY!

Blake: Equality!

Tyler: Equality!

10 Kyle: Hell yeah, dude! Equality!

Jared: Manny? You with us, bro?

Everyone: [. . .]

Manny: Course I am, bro. Equality!

CLINK[4]*!*

1 brethren [ˈbreðrən]: *Brüder*; old-fashioned expression used to talk to people in church or to talk about the members of a male religious group 2 content (n): essence, meaning 3 Perrier [ˈpɛrɪeɪ]: a sparkling mineral water from France 4 clink (n): sound made by glasses being knocked together

September 18

DEAR MARTIN,

I just got back to school after an impromptu[1] trip to the hood[2]. Putting all my cards on the table[3], I went home with the intention[4] of just staying there forever (which is extreme, I know).   5

When I got there, Mama was curled up[5] on the couch with her nose buried[6] in How Stella Got Her Groove Back. Just seeing her reading, something she worked hard to teach me to do, I knew I'd be on the bus back to school before the evening was over.

"Whatchu[7] doin' here, boy? It's a school night" was the first thing 10 she said (without looking up from the book).

"Can't I drop[8] in to see my dear ol'[9] mom when I'm missin' her?"

"Who you callin' old?"

That made me laugh.

"You gonna tell me what's really going on?" She closed the book and 15 put it to the side then.

I dropped my bag with a sigh[10]. "Just been a rough few weeks."

"Come on over here and sit down."

In all honesty, I didn't want to. *Sit down* is Mama-code for "spit it out," and I woulda preferred to get my big toes shot off than talk 20 about the stuff I was trying to escape. But Mama being Mama—and possibly psychic?—she pulled it right outta[11] me. "This about that cop and them[12] handcuffs?"

I dropped down beside her. "Little bit. I keep thinking about how much worse it coulda gone."   25

---

1 impromptu [ɪmˈprɑːmptuː]: spontaneous **2** hood (sl): neighborhood
3 put your cards on the table: tell the truth about your plans **4** intention: goal, plan **5** curl up: sit comfortably on a chair or sofa with your legs up under you
6 bury [ˈberi]: (here) have a book so close to your face that your nose is almost between the pages **7** whatchu (infml): what are you **8** drop in: visit **9** ol' (infml): old **10** sigh (v): breathe out heavily **11** outta (infml): out of **12** them (infml): those

"That non-indictment in the Carson case got you shook[1], huh?"

"Yeah. We had this discussion in class today, and . . .

I don't know, Ma. Everything I'm doing right now feels like a losing battle."

5 She nodded. "Hard being a black man, ain't it[2]?"

I shrugged[3]. "Guess that's one way to put it. All I know is I can't seem to find where I fit. Especially at that school."

"Hmm."

"It's just like . . . I've been there my whole high school career, and I still
10 feel like an outsider, you know? We were talking about the Declaration of Independence, and all I could think was how Shemar Carson was straight-up[4] denied his 'inalienable[5] rights.' It really bugged me out."

"It should've."

"I did the math when I got back to my room: there were 192 years
15 between the Declaration of Independence and the end of all that Jim Crow[6] stuff. Now we're over a decade[7] into the twenty-first century, and I know from experience people like me are still getting shafted[8]."

Mama nodded. "Mmhmm."

"Sittin' there listenin' to this rich white boy brag[9] about breaking the
20 law after I sat in handcuffs for no reason . . . I can't even tell you how hard that was, Ma. It's like no matter what I do, I can't win."

She crossed her arms and lifted her chin, and that's when I knew there'd be no sympathy. "So whatchu gon'[10] do? Run away?"

I sighed. "I don't know, Mama."

25 "You think coming back here will solve your problem?"

"At least I'd be around people who know the struggle."

She snorted. "Boy, you betta[11] get your behind[12] on up to that school."

"But, Ma—"

---

1 to get sb. shook: to upset sb. **2** ain't it (infml): (here) isn't it **3** shrug (v): move your shoulders up and down to show that you are not sure **4** straight-up: truly, honestly **5** inalienable rights: rights that cannot be taken away **6** Jim Crow: laws in force in the Southern US until 1968 that kept Black people separated from white people **7** decade: a period of ten years **8** shaft (v): treat sb. unfairly **9** brag about: talk in a very proud way **10** gon' (infml): going to **11** betta (infml): had better (should) **12** behind (infml): bottom, backside

"Don't 'But, Ma' me, Justyce."

"I don't fit there, though, Mama."

"I've been tellin' you since you were small that you gotta[1] make a place for yourself in this world," she said. "You thought I was playin'[2]?"

I sighed again.   5

"You ever consider that maybe you not supposed to 'fit'? People who make history rarely do."

"Aww, here we go with this 'making history' thing again."

"Goodbye, Justyce. I didn't raise you to punk out[3] when the going gets rough[4]. Get on outta here." She picked up her book.   10

"Dang, I can't even get a hug? Somethin' to eat?"

"You know where the kitchen is. You can get a hug on your way out."

See what I deal with, Martin?

On the return trip, it really hit me hard: she's right. There's really nowhere to run. While it's been hard processing[5] my arrest/Castillo's   15 death/the Carson case/ dealing with fools like Jared and them on the daily[6] without getting discouraged[7], when it comes down to it[8], I don't really have an alternative but to keep going, do I?

I'll tell you the hardest thing for me today: sitting in the lounge listening to Manny agree with those fools. Granted[9], I could tell his heart   20 wasn't in it . . .

But still.

I'll be candid[10] with you: sometimes it really bugs[11] me that Manny spends so much time with those guys. I know he's known them forever, and it's none of my business, but it's hard to see my boy hang out with   25 dudes who are blatantly[12] disrespectful to our people. (Who puts a little kid in blackface[13]?!) And then he doesn't say anything about it? I guess it's possible it doesn't bother him, but to hear him agree that things are

---

1 gotta (infml): have got to **2** play (v) (infml): (here) not be serious, joke
3 punk out: give up **4** the going gets rough: sth. gets difficult **5** process (v): deal
with **6** on the daily (infml): every day **7** discouraged [dɪsˈkɜːrɪdʒd]: without hope
8 come down to sth.: depend on one important point **9** granted: indeed,
accepted **10** candid: honest **11** bug (v): annoy **12** blatant: carried out openly
13 blackface (n): practice of a white person wearing dark make-up to appear as a
Black person; once common on stage, TV, etc. it is now taboo

equal when he KNOWS about my incident . . . well, I'm kinda[1] mad about that, if you want the truth.

I've been trying to figure out what you would've done if you'd been in my shoes today. I know you lived in a world where black folks were hosed[2] and beaten and jailed and killed while fighting for equal rights, but you still managed to be, like, dignified[3] and everything.

How did you do that, Martin? How do I do that? There are people who don't see a man with rights when they look at me, and I'm not real sure how to deal with that.

Being treated the way I was and then hearing Jared insist[4] there's not a problem? And then hearing Manny agree with him? It sucks[5], Martin. It really does.

So what do I do now? How do I handle people like Jared? Arguing[6] obviously won't work Do I just ignore him? But what does that solve, Martin? I want to "put my best foot forward[7]," as Mama would say. That's what you did. Just gotta figure out how. . . .

Time to knock out[8] some of this homework. Hopefully I can focus.

Thanks for hearing me out,
Justyce

---

1 kinda (infml): kind of **2** hose (v): (here) spray large amounts of water powerfully against people to stop them demonstrating **3** dignified ['dɪgnɪfaɪd]: honorable **4** insist: say strongly that sth. is true **5** suck (AE) (v) (infml): be very bad **6** argue: disagree **7** put your best foot forward: make a lot of effort to achieve sth. **8** knock sth. out: produce sth. quickly

CHAPTER 5

The minute Jared, Kyle, Tyler, and Blake step into Manny's basement, it's clear Jared's Equality Brigade[1] thing was a terrible idea.

In the month and a half since the racial equality discussion in Socio Evo, Jared's been on a crusade[2] to prove things in America are equal. Last week, he told Manny and his crew about this *brilliant-ass idea* he had: "Bros," he said, "let's all dress as different stereotypes for Halloween, and then go out *together*. It'll be this massive political statement about racial equality and broken barriers and shit." Dude even asked Justyce to participate.

Jus, of course, wasn't real keen[3] at first . . . but he let Manny talk him into it.

He's regretting[4] that now.

Five of the six costumes are mostly fine. Jus is the Thug, naturally: pants belted[5] around his thighs[6] with boxers exposed[7], Thug Life T-shirt, thick gold chain with a huge medallion, fitted flat-billed[8] baseball cap. He and Manny even made a grill[9] out of a gum wrapper[10] for Jus to wear on his bottom[11] teeth.

Manny's the Token Black Guy: khakis[12], loafers[13], and polo with a cable-knit[14] sweater draped[15] over his shoulders and tied loosely[16]

---

1 brigade [brɪˈɡeɪd]: group of people who share the same opinions 2 crusade [kruːˈseɪd] (n): long effort to achieve sth. 3 keen: enthusiastic 4 regret (v): feel upset with yourself for doing or not doing sth. 5 belted: held up with a (leather) belt 6 thigh: leg above the knee, below the hip 7 expose: show sth. that is hidden 8 bill (n): (here) the hard front part of a baseball cap which sticks out 9 grill (n): (here) jewelry for teeth 10 gum wrapper: piece of paper around a chewing gum 11 bottom: lower 12 khaki: type of trousers 13 loafers: flat leather shoes 14 cable-knit: a knitted pattern used in clothes that looks like cables twisted around each other 15 drape (v): hang sth. over/on sth. else 16 tied loosely: bound together in a loose way

at the chest. He's really into it too: as soon as he was dressed, he started calling Jus "old chap[1]" and "my good man."

Jared's the Yuppie[2]/Politician. He's wearing a suit[3] . . . even has a spot on his chin where he nicked[4] himself shaving and left the little
5 piece of tissue there "for effect."

Tyler's the Surfer Dude: board shorts and a tank top even though it's only fifty degrees[5] out.

Kyle went with the Redneck[6]: woodland camouflage[7] shirt, overalls, trucker hat with a Confederate flag[8] patch[9], dingy[10] cowboy
10 boots. He even had his sister attach a few of her hair extensions so he has a mullet[11]. Frankly, this one is toeing[12] the line, but okay. Not quite crossing it.

Blake, though? Blake takes it too far[13]. He's dressed as a Klansman[14]. He's got on the white robe with the circular[15] red and white
15 cross patch on the chest, and he even has the pointed[16] hood with the eyeholes cut out. If Jus didn't know it was a costume, he'd be a little scared.

"J . . . uhh . . . can I talk to you for a sec, dawg?" Manny says to Jared, who, to Justyce's surprise, also seems pretty uncomfortable
20 with Blake's choice of attire[17].

"Sure, man."

---

1 chap (n): man/boy **2** yuppie (AE) (infml) (derog): young professional with money living in the city (young urban professional) **3** suit (n): formal or business clothing with matching top and bottom **4** nick (v): make a small cut **5** degrees Fahrenheit: temperature scale used in the US (50° F = 10° C) **6** redneck (AE) (infml) (derog): stereotype of the uneducated, unmannered white person from the countryside **7** camouflage ['kæməflɑːʒ] (n): coloured in a way to not be seen easily **8** Confederate Flag: flag representing the Confederate States of America who tried to leave the United Sates in order to keep their right to own slaves and caused the American Civil War (1861–1865) **9** patch (n): piece of material to cover a hole **10** dingy ['dɪndʒi]: old and damaged **11** mullet: hairstyle (short at the front and sides and long at the back) **12** toe the line: behave in a way an authority tells you to **13** take sth. too far: behave in an unacceptable way **14** Klansman: member of the Ku Klux Klan, a secret organization of extreme, violent, racist white men **15** circular ['sɜːrkjələr]: having a shape like a circle **16** pointed: having a sharp end **17** attire (n): clothing

They walk to Manny's room, and Justyce is left standing with the others.

"Justyce, that costume is *sick*, homie!" Blake says. (Because a Klansman would definitely call a black guy *homie*.) Jus fights the urge to shake his head. "Yours is . . . uhh . . ."   5

"Wait till I put the hood on, bro. This right here is the genuine[1] article." He spreads his arms, beaming[2] like he's wrapped[3] in a garment[4] formerly worn by Jesus. Justyce is tempted[5] to ask where the "genuine article" came from, but he's not sure he wants to know the answer.

Just then, Jared reappears[6]. "Hey, Justyce, Manny wants to talk   10 to you, bro."

Justyce nods and takes the deepest breath he's ever taken, then strides[7] to Manny's room with eight white-boy eyes burning into him like lasers.

Yeah, this blows[8].   15

"'Sup[9], dawg?" Jus says once he steps in and closes Manny's door. (Though of course he already knows what it's about.)

"So Blake's costume is . . . Well, you saw it."

Jus snorts. "I did."

"If you . . . umm"—Manny scratches[10] his neck—"don't wanna go   20 anymore—"

"It's cool, Manny."

Manny's thick[11] eyebrows jump to the sky. "It is?"

"Yeah, man." Truth is, four hours ago, Jus was ready to back out[12] because the idea of going *anywhere* with Jared and crew just felt   25 wrong, knowing what he knows about how they think. But then he stumbled[13] upon Martin's definition of integration—"intergroup and interpersonal living"—and decided to just go with it. He's not

---

1 genuine [ˈdʒenjuɪn]: authentic **2** beam (v): have a big smile on your face
3 wrap (v): fold paper or cloth around sth. **4** garment: clothing **5** tempted to do
sth.: have the wish to do sth. that you shouldn't **6** reappear: come back
7 stride (v): walk with long steps **8** blow (v) (infml): be very bad **9** 'sup (infml):
what's up **10** scratch (v): rub your fingernails against your skin **11** thick: wide
12 back out: no longer take part in sth. **13** stumble upon: discover unexpectedly

sure this is exactly what Martin meant, but what is he supposed to say? "You ready to go, dawg?"

"Oh." Manny clears his throat. "I guess so."

"Let's roll[1], then." Jus leaves the room. It's just a costume, right?
5 Brotherhood for the win.

As soon as Jus and Manny get back to the others, Jared takes a bunch of group pictures and posts them online. Then he says, "Equality Brigade, let's ride," and leads the charge to the door.

When they get to Manny's car and Blake pulls on the hood and
10 raises his arm in the Nazi salute[2], Justyce knows the train he just hopped on is headed downhill[3] in a major way. It occurs[4] to him that the moment he said he was cool with the whole thing, he cut the brake lines[5] and completely surrendered[6] his power to stop it.

And he's right.
15 Not five minutes after they get to the party, somebody sucker-punches[7] Blake in the face. The burst[8] of bright red beneath the eye-holes in his pointed hood makes Justyce sick to his stomach.

The next thing he knows, there's a group of *genuinely* thugged-out black dudes—and one white guy—standing in front of the Equality
20 Brigade, looking like they wanna break ALL of their stereotype faces.

The worst part? Justyce knows every single one of them. They live in his mom's neighborhood. This is Manny's cousin's crew. Jus is pretty sure they all belong to a gang called the Black Jihad run by a crazy older dude named Martel Montgomery.
25 A dark-skinned guy with short dreadlocks gives Jus a once-over[9] and smiles. "That's a real funny costume, Justyce."

"Oh ... uhhh ... thanks, Trey." (Definitely not Jus's most valiant[10] moment.)

"And you ...," Trey says to Manny. "You Quan cousin, right?"

---

1 let's roll (infml): let's go **2** Nazi salute (n): *Hitlergruß* **3** downhill (adj): going down **4** occur to sb.: suddenly think of sth. **5** cut the brake lines: make the brake not function anymore **6** surrender (v): give up **7** sucker-punch: hit sb. who is not expecting it **8** burst (n): explosion **9** give sb. a once-over (infml): look at sb. from head to toe **10** valiant ['væliənt]: courageous, brave

"Yeah," Manny says, scratching the back of his neck.

"The fuck y'all doin' here with these assclowns[1], bruh[2]? Just gon' letcha[3] boy disrespect our people like that?" Trey points to Blake, who has removed his pointed hood and is holding it to his nose to stanch[4] the bleeding.   5

Jared: Dude, we didn't mean you any disrespect—

Manny: Chill, Jared.

Trey: Yeah, *Jared.* You should really shut ya mouth right now. Your boy has made me and my dudes upset coming in here dressed like that.   10

Justyce: Trey, he didn't mean anything by it, dawg. We were doing this satire thing with stereotypes, and it went too far. Lesson learned.

Trey smiles at Justyce then. Well, more like sneers[5]. It makes Jus feel like cockroaches[6] are walking all over him. "You ain't[7] changed a bit, Justyce. Still Mr. Smarty-Pants[8]," Trey says, and then one of the   15
others pipes up: "Y'all know he goes to that rich-ass white school out in Oak Ridge now."

"It's called Braselton Prep," Jared corrects. Justyce really wants Jared to shut the hell up.

"Ooooh." The white dude—Brad, Jus believes—raises his hands   20
in mock[9] adoration[10].

Trey looks back and forth between Jus and Manny. "Don't get it twisted, my dawgs. These white boys might be standing here next to y'all, but y'all still ain't[11] nothin' but niggas[12] to them, ya heard me?" he says. "Ain't no amount of money nor intelligence can change that   25
shit."

Jared: Hey, man, that's not true. You don't ev—

"Shut UP, Jared!" (This from Surfer-Tyler.) "Let's just leave, bro."

1 assclown (AE) (sl): silly and embarrassing person **2** bruh (sl): brother
3 letcha (infml): let your **4** stanch sth. [stɑːntʃ] (AE): stop the flow of sth., esp.
blood **5** sneer (v): look at sb. with disrespect **6** cockroach: *Kakerlake*
7 ain't (infml): (here) haven't **8** Mr Smarty-Pants (infml, derog): person who
thinks he/she is clever, know-it-all **9** mock (adj): fake, not honest **10** adoration:
feeling of great love **11** ain't (infml): (here) aren't **12** nigga (sl, derog): very
offensive word for a Black person

Trey: Sounds like a great idea to me.

Jared: Bro, this isn't even your party. You can't tell us to leave.

Trey laughs, and one of the other guys lifts[1] his shirt to reveal[2] the handgun grip sticking[3] out of his waistband[4].

5   "I most certainly can, white boy," Trey says. "Now you and ya li'l[5] crew getcha[6] punk asses outta here before things escalate[7]."

The guy with the gun smiles at Jus. "You and rich boy can stay with us if you want to." All the Black Jihad guys laugh.

Trey: Bruh, you know these niggas don't wanna chill with us.
10 They "goin places" and shit. Gotta[8] stay connected to the white man for the ride to the top. . . .

He nudges[9] the white guy with them, and they both snicker.

"Let's go, y'all," Jus says.

As they turn to leave, Justyce can feel Manny trying to catch his
15 attention, but he stares straight ahead. They step outside and the chilly[10] night air hits their faces. Jus hears Jared ask Manny, "You all right, bro?"

"Yeah, man. I'm cool," Manny replies[11].

Jared steps ahead to talk to the others, and Jus watches Manny
20 examine his tied sweater, his khakis, his loafers—his "costume" made up of clothes he pulled from his closet. He unties the sweater, then looks up at Justyce.

For the moment, they understand each other.

Justyce takes the fitted cap from his head and the fake chain
25 from his neck.

"Happy Halloween, muthafuckas[12]!" Trey calls out behind them.

---

1 lift (v): move upwards 2 reveal (v): show, uncover 3 stick out: easily seen,
stand out 4 waistband: belt, string 5 li'l (infml): little 6 getcha (infml): get your
7 escalate [eskəleɪt]: become greater, worse, more serious 8 gotta (infml): got to
9 nudge (v): push gently 10 chilly: cold 11 reply (v): answer 12 muthafucka
(sl) (derog): motherfucker, insult

November 1

DEAR MARTIN,

It's 2 a.m. and I just got off the phone with SJ.

Which is crazy.

Started out innocently enough . . . When I got to my room at   5
10:15 p.m., I had a missed call from her. I figured it had to do with
debate stuff since the state tournament is around the corner, so I decided
to hit[1] her back. Here's how it went down:

SJ: Hello?

Me: Hey, SJ. It's Justyce. You called?   10

SJ: Caller ID[2], Jus. No need to announce yourself.

Me: Oh. Okay.

SJ: (Laughs.) I was just calling to see how Douche-Nugget[3] Christensen's experiment-at-you-and-Manny's-expense[4] went. I saw the pics
he posted and had to go for a run to keep from showing up at the party   15
and punching[5] Blake in the face.

Me: Yeah, no worries about that. Somebody did it for you.

SJ: Shut up! Someone punched him for real?

Me: Ruined his pointed hood.

SJ: (Laughs so hard I think she's going to choke[6].)   20

Me: So . . . how was your night?

---

1 hit sb. back (infml): (here) phone sb. back **2** caller ID: the number and name
of the person calling you is shown on the phone display **3** douche-nugget [duːʃ
ˈnʌgɪt] (AE) (infml, derog): arrogant, rude person **4** at sb.'s expense: with loss or
damage to somebody **5** punch (v): hit **6** choke [tʃəʊk] (v): to be unable to
breathe properly (because you cannot get enough air)

SJ: Uneventful[1]. I spent most of it thinking about you.

Me: . . .

SJ: I mean . . . um. Sorry, that came out wrong.

Me: . . .

5 SJ: Jus, are you still there? God, I'm such an idiot . . .

Me: (Clears throat.) I'm here.

SJ: Whew[2]. Okay, good.

Me and SJ: (Awkward[3] pause.)

Me: So, um . . . how was it supposed to come out[4]?

10 SJ: Well . . . I just meant because of the costumes? Like I saw the pictures, and was wondering how things were going at the party.

Me: Ah.

SJ: You don't believe me, do you?

Me: Why wouldn't I? (Even though in my head I was like, "Hell nah, I
15 don't believe you, girl.")

SJ: (Laughs.) I certainly wouldn't believe me.

Me: . . .

SJ: I have to say, I'm enjoying this rendering[5]-Justyce-McAllister-speechless[6] thing. Maybe I should say this kind of stuff more often.

20 Me: Shut up.

SJ: (Laughs some more.) So how are you, anyway?

Me: What do you mean?

---

1 uneventful: boring **2** whew [hwjuː]: sound of surprise **3** awkward [ˈɔːkwərd]: embarrassing, unpleasant **4** come out: be said **5** render: cause sb. to be in a certain situation **6** speechless: not able to talk

SJ: I'm sure the whole party thing was awkward, no?

Me: That's one way to put it, I guess.

[No clue[1] why, but I tell SJ every detail about the party.]

SJ: Wow. So they threatened you with a gun to get you to go?

Me: Yep.   5

SJ: That's pretty intense, Jus.

Me: Tell me about it. Craziest part is I still feel weird about leaving.

SJ: You do? Why?

Me: Well, either way it went, I was sayin somethin', you know? Staying woulda[2] been a statement of solidarity[3] with these guys I grew up   10
with—and who look like me. Leaving was a different statement, and
the fact that I chose to do it with a white guy who was dressed as a
Klansman . . . well . . .

SJ: Hmm. I see what you mean.

Me: Yeah. These were the dudes who used to call me White Boy because   15
while they were shooting dice[4] for pennies[5] at recess[6], I was reading a
book. I know there's no excuse for the idea that we're all the same "kind,"
as that cop Castillo put it, but the moment I saw that gun sticking out
of dude's waistband, I felt this flare[7] of pain around my wrists. I had this
thought—be forewarned, it's an ugly one: it's assholes like Trey and his   20
boys that have cops thinking all black dudes are up to no good.

SJ: I'm so sorry, Jus.

Me: Don't apologize, S. It's not your fault. It never made sense to me
why tryna[8] DO something with myself made me some kind of race-

---

1 clue (n): idea, hint **2** woulda (infml): would have **3** solidarity: support by one
person/group for another **4** shoot dice: play a game with dice **5** penny: cent
6 recess (v): break **7** flare (n): breakout, spread **8** tryna (infml): trying to

traitor[1] to these guys, but some of the stuff Trey said tonight really got
to me.

SJ: Really?

Me: Yeah. He said me and Manny were chillin' with Jared and them
5 because we "need the white man for the ride to the top." And while I
could debate that till I'm blue in the face[2], didn't we prove it by leaving
with Jared and them?

SJ: I guess that's one way to look at it.

Me: What if Trey is right? What if, no matter what[3] I do, the only thing
10 white people will ever see me as is a nig—an "n-word"?

(So glad I caught myself, Martin.)

Me (cont.): Yeah, Jared's always talking about how "equal" things are,
but that doesn't mean he sees me as one.

SJ: (Silence.)

15 Me: It's a conundrum[4]: white people hold most positions of authority
in this country. How do I deal with the fact that I DO need them to
get ahead[5] without feeling like I'm turning my back on my own people?

SJ: Sure hope that's rhetorical[6], Jus. I certainly can't give you an answer.

Me: (Laughs.)

---

1 traitor: sb. who is not loyal and faithful **2** do sth. till you are blue in the face
(infml): try as hard as you can without success **3** no matter what: sth. is always
true, in every situation **4** conundrum [kəˈnʌndrəm]: mystery, puzzle **5** get
ahead: be successful **6** rhetorical [rɪˈtɔːrɪkl]: said or asked to make a statement
without expecting an answer

We shifted gears[1] a little bit after that, and when I checked the clock, it'd been three hours. When we landed on the topic of Jewish[2] involvement[3] in the civil rights movement[4], I wound up telling her about this Be Like Martin experiment. She said she was "both impressed[5] and intrigued[6]."

That's when it hit me who I was talkin' to and I said I needed to go to bed.

Before we hung up[7], though? She said something I don't think I'll ever forget:

SJ: Hey, Jus?

Me: Yeah?

SJ: I want to apologize.

Me: For what?

SJ: For stepping out of line in class a while back.

Me: . . .

SJ: I know it's been over a month, but after talking to you tonight . . . Well, it wasn't my place to speak for you. I'm really, really sorry.

Hearing her apologize after Blake didn't? It got me, Martin. Now I can't get her out of my head.

---

1 shift gears: (here) change the topic **2** Jewish: relating to the religion of Judaism or Jewish people **3** involvement: participation **4** civil rights movement: campaign in the US in order to allow African Americans the same rights as others (1950s/60s) **5** impressed: fascinated **6** intrigued [ɪnˈtriːgd]: attracted, very interested in sth./sb. **7** hang up: end a conversation on the phone

Which really isn't good.

Don't get me wrong: SJ's great. We've been debate partners since I joined the team two years ago. Only person at that school who knows more about me than she does is Manny.

5   Yes, she's gorgeous for a white girl—she's tall with long brown hair, and while not a big-booty[1] Betty, the lacrosse body is tight.

Yes, she's smart and funny and easy to talk to and kinda feisty[2]— which now that I'm seeing her in this new light is kind of a turn-on . . .

But, Martin, I can't fall for SJ! My whole life, Mama's told me,
10 "Don't you bring home a white girl." We're talking about a woman who low-key[3] disses[4] Melo for looking white. Can you imagine what kind of reaction I'd get if it were SJ? (Melo and I broke up again, by the way.)

Right now, I feel guilty for even talking to SJ. Especially about race stuff! What does it say about me that I willingly left a party with a
15 bunch of idiots, but the white person who does treat me as an equal is the one I most wanna run away from right now? I can't believe I told SJ all that stuff! I mean, she's cool and everything but . . . I'm shaking my head right now.

You were the man, Martin. THE man. And I wanna be like you.
20 "Intergroup and interpersonal living"? I really do want that . . .

I'm just not so sure I can pull it off[5] anymore.

I'm going to bed.

—JM

---

1 booty (infml): part of the body that you sit on **2** feisty: *quirlig* **3** low-key: quietly, privately **4** dis sb. (infml): say bad things about sb. **5** pull sth. off: succeed at doing sth.

CHAPTER 6

Justyce can't believe it.

CONGRATULATIONS! is all big and bright right there in front of him, but he still can't believe it.

When he sat down at his laptop, he expected to have to click a bunch of different links to get to his admissions[1] decision, but the second he logged in to the website, a giant bulldog filled the screen as the Yale fight song played all loud and bold[2] and beautiful.

His phone is in his hand now, and he's tapping.

She picks up on the first ring:

"Hello?"

"S?"

"Jus? Is everything okay?"

"S, I got in."

"What?"

"I got in, SJ!"

"What are you talki—Wait . . . you got IN?"

"YES!"

"Like, GOT IN, got in? Like you're IN?"

"YES!"

"OHMYGOD, OHMYGOD, OHMYGOD!"

Justyce reads the computer screen again, and it really hits him.

"S, YA BOY IS A YALIE[3]!"

"HOLY SHIT, JUS. HOLY SHIT!"

"I can't even believe it." Jus drops his head back and closes his eyes. All the bad stuff that's happened in the past few months falls away.

---

1 admission: accepting sb. into an institution, e.g. college **2** bold (adj): strong, clear **3** Yalie (AE) (infml): sb. attending Yale University

After a pause, he hears, "Mom, Dad, Jus is going to Yale!" and then: "Wow! Congratulations, Justyce!" (from SJ's mom) and "Attaboy[1], Jusmeister[2]!" (from SJ's dad—who's been calling him that since the first time he showed up at SJ's house to work on debate stuff).

5 "AAAAACK[3]! JUS! This is the best Hanukkah[4] present ever! You realize this means we'll only be an hour and a half away from each other, right?"

That's when it smacks him again.

The *feeling.*

10 The one that makes his heart beat faster and his head go fuzzy when he's talking to her sometimes. It's different from how he felt about Melo . . . and that's what scares Jus. It occurs to him that he dialed[5] SJ before he called his mama. Which says *way* more than he wants to hear right now.

15 "S, I gotta go," he says.

"Okay! I'll see you tomorrow. I'm so EXCITED!"

Justyce smiles, very much in spite[6] of himself. "Me too." Yeah, this has to stop.

"Thanks for calling to share the news," she says. "Means a lot to
20 me that you did."

"Means a lot to *me* that you're so amped[7]."

(Damn, prolly shouldn't have said that.)

"Are you kidding? How could I not be?"

Justyce clears his throat. "I hope you have a nice night, SJ."

25 "You too, Jus. Sweet dreams."

But Justyce doesn't dream at all. He can't sleep. Too much on his mind.

Yale, for one. (Hello, *dream come true!*)

And then SJ. *How could I not be?* she said.

---

1 attaboy (infml): expression to show admiration or encouragement for a male person **2** -meister: referring to sb. who is very good at sth. **3** ack (infml): short for acknowledgement, realizing that sth. is true **4** Hanukkah: Jewish festival **5** dial (v): phone **6** do sth. in spite of yourself: do sth. although you did not expect it **7** amped: excited

What is he supposed to do with that?

He called Mama as soon as he and SJ hung up, but it went to voice mail. And since he couldn't bring himself to leave such big news in a message, he went to bed with the weight of SJ knowing before Mama on his chest. ⁵

The next morning, he's standing near the omelet station in the dining hall when he hears his name shouted from across the room.

It's her. And she's *bounding*[1] in his direction.

"S!" Justyce shouts, throwing his arms wide without thinking. She leaps into them and wraps her legs around his waist. It's . . . a lot. ¹⁰

She's also in uniform, which means . . . "S, you know you're in a skirt, right?"

"Crap[2]!" She scrambles down. "Oh my god, I'm so embarrassed[3]." Her face is all red, so she covers it with her hands.

It might be the cutest thing Jus has ever seen. ¹⁵

He pulls her hands down. Smiles. "That was prolly the best hug I've ever gotten in my life."

She shakes her head. "I can't believe I *attacked* you. I just got so excited."

Jus laughs. "Me too, S. Hope you'll come see ya boy every now ²⁰ and then. I'll definitely come see you."

You would think Jus had just proposed[4], the way SJ's face lights up. He should *not* be saying this kinda stuff . . . And he definitely shouldn't be meaning it.

She smiles. ²⁵

He smiles back.

She stares.

He stares back.

He realizes he's still holding her hands and looks at her lips—

"Umm . . . Hey, Jus." ³⁰

Jus's head snaps to the right.

---

1 bound (v): run or jump excitedly **2** crap (n): oh no, shit **3** embarrassed: feeling shy and uncomfortable in a public situation **4** propose to sb.: ask sb. to marry you

Melo.

He snatches his hands away from SJ's. "Uhh . . ."

When he turns back to SJ, her smile is melting off her face.

He watches Melo's green eyes shift back and forth between him
5 and SJ. SJ's smile has melted so thoroughly, it's officially a scowl[1].

Melo clears her throat.

"Oh, uhh . . . 'Sup, Melo?" Jus says.

"I was hoping you could tell me, Justyce." Except her eyes are on
SJ.

10 No one speaks.

Then: "Okay! Umm . . . Guess I'll see you in class?" SJ says.
Tongue-tied[2], Justyce watches her pivot[3] and walk away without
looking back.

When he faces Melo again, she's smirking[4] in SJ's direction.
15 Justyce coughs to get Melo's attention.

She turns to him and crosses her arms. "So I hear you got into
Yale," she says.

"Yeah, I did."

"That what SJ was so excited about?"

20 "Yeah." Justyce gulps. "She's going to Columbia. It's pretty close
by."

Melo shifts her focus to the doorway SJ disappeared through. "So
you two are a thing now?"

"What? No!"

25 "I saw her jump on you, Justyce."

"It's not like that, Mel."

Except it is, obviously.

"We're just good friends," he says to the air. "Debate partners. You
know what I mean."

30 "Good." She takes a step closer. He can tell she's not convinced,
but that's the thing about Melo: if she wants something, she'll do

---

1 scowl [skaʊl] (v): look at sb. in an angry way **2** tongue-tied: not able to say sth.
because of nervousness or feeling shy **3** pivot ['pɪvət] (v): change direction
4 smirk [smɜːrk] (v): smile in an unpleasant way

whatever it takes to get it. "I was hoping we could hang out soon."
She runs a finger down the center of Justyce's chest and hooks[1] it
into the waistband of his pants.

"Uhh, yeah." His voice cracks and everything. "That'd, uhh . . .
That'd be cool."   5

"Awesome. I'm actually pretty sad you're gonna be leaving me.
You sure you wanna go so far away?"

Jus shifts his attention over her shoulder and scratches his head.

"I'll call you later, okay?"

"Aiight[2]," Jus says.   10

She squeezes his biceps and kisses him in the little nook[3] where
his jawbone meets his neck. "Bye, Jus."

Jus doesn't say a word. Just stares at Melo's butt as she saunters[4]
off.

---

1 hook (v): put your finger around sth. else **2** aiight (infml): alright **3** nook: a
small place **4** saunter ['sɔːntər] (v): walk in a slow and relaxed way

CHAPTER 7

Justyce is still in a daze[1] when he gets to Societal Evolution two periods later. He knows he messed up—just can't figure out exactly what went wrong with which girl.

When he steps into the classroom, Manny comes forward and
5   drapes an arm around his shoulders. "Dr. Dray, allow me to introduce you to Justyce McAllister, soon-to-be Yale undergrad[2] and my very best friend."

"My man!" Doc says, lifting his hand for a high five. "That's what I'm talkin' about!"

10   It makes Justyce smile.

Unfortunately, the minute he takes his seat, SJ comes in and won't even look at him. And hot on her heels[3] is Jared Christensen, who glares so intensely, it's a wonder Jus's head doesn't burst into flames.

15   The bell rings, and Doc closes the door and turns around to face the class, but before he can say "Good morning," Jared's hand is in the air.

Doc: Yes, Mr. Christensen?

Jared: I have something I'd like to discuss today, sir.

20   Doc: Okay . . . Let's hear it.

Jared: I'd like to discuss how affirmative action[4] discriminates against members of the majority.

---

1 in a daze: feeling confused **2** undergrad: undergraduate, university student studying for their first degree **3** hot on sb.'s heels: close behind sb. **4** affirmative action [əˌfɜːrmətɪv ˈækʃn] (AE): the practice or policy of making sure a certain number of jobs, college places, etc. are given to people from minority groups or groups that have been treated unfairly in the past

Justyce: [*Eyebrows rise.*]

SJ: You're not even serious.

Jared: Oh, I certainly am. Let's observe, shall we? I'm ranked number two in our class, I'm captain of the baseball team, I do community service[1] on weekends, and I got higher test scores than Justyce ... yet he got into Yale early 5 action[2], and I didn't. I know for a fact it's because I'm white and he's black.

Doc: That's quite an assumption[3], Mr. Christensen—

Justyce: Hold up ... what makes you so sure you got higher scores than me?

Jared: Dude, I got a fifteen-eighty on the SAT.

Manny: What'd you get, Jus?   10

Justyce: Fifteen-sixty.

Jared: See?

SJ: What about the ACT?

Jared: Thirty-three.

SJ: Jus?   15

Justyce: Thirty-four.

Jared: Bullshit!

Doc: Watch it, Jared.

Jared: Dude, there's no way he got a thirty-four.

Justyce: What reason do I have to lie, man?   20

Jared: It just doesn't make sense—

---

1 community service: unpaid work in the local neighborhood **2** early action: plan to allow students to apply and gain admission to a college earlier than others **3** assumption [ə'sʌmpʃn]: belief (without proof) that sth. is true or will happen

Justyce: Why doesn't it?

SJ: Because it negates[1] his assumption that because he's white and you're black, he's more intelligent than you are.

Jared: Why don't you stay out[2] of it, SJ?

5 Jus: Hold up, man—

Doc: This is an open forum[3], Mr. Christensen. Anyone in this room can contribute[4] to the discussion.

Jared: Whatever.

Manny: So let me get this straight,

10 J: It bugs you that Justyce is just as smart as you?

Jared: That's not my point.

SJ: You said affirmative action "discriminates against members of the majority," and you cited Jus's acceptance to Yale and your lack thereof as supporting evidence for that assertion. Ignoring how effing[5] racist it is to
15 assume your test scores would be higher than Justyce's, the counterevidence[6]—namely that you and Justyce are more or less equally qualified—has nullified[7] your assertion.

Jared: It doesn't nullify anything.

Justyce: [*Shakes his head.*]

20 Jared: If we're equals, we *both* should've gotten in.

Manny: You got rejected?

Jared: . . . Deferred[8].

---

1 negate: make another thing lose its effect **2** stay out of sth.: not get involved with sth. **3** forum: place or group where people can exchange ideas **4** contribute to sth.: speak during a meeting or discussion not having sth.
5 effing (infml): used instead of "fucking" **6** counterevidence: proof that another proof is wrong **7** nullify sth. ['nʌlɪfaɪ]: make sth. lose its power or force
8 defer sth.: *etwas zurückstellen*

SJ: So you'll probably still get in—

Jared: That's not the point!

Doc: Let's keep it professional, Mr. Christensen.

Manny: For real, J. Chill.

Jared: No, dude. I'm not going to "chill." You of all people should know what   5
kinda shit I caught from my dad for getting deferred.

Manny: That doesn't have anything to do with Jus, though, man.

Jared: Yeah it does. He took a spot[1] *I* didn't get because Yale has to fill a
quota[2]—

Justyce: Excuse me?   10

Jared: Just stating the facts, man.

SJ: Those aren't facts, dipshit[3].

Doc: Sarah-Jane . . .

SJ: Justyce got in because he deserved to.

Justyce: Thank you.   15

Jared: I deserved to get in too! Affirmative action is bullshit.

Doc: If y'all can't reel this in, I'm shutting it down. Final warning.

Jared: Point is, it gives an unfair advantage to minorities. So, okay, Justyce
and I might be "equals" or whatever. But there are other minorities without
the qualifications I have who will get in before I do. That's just not fair.   20

SJ: Jared, let me ask you something.

Jared: Like I have another option.

---

1 spot (n): place   **2** quota: (here) certain amount of places kept for minority
candidates only   **3** dipshit (AE) (sl): stupid person

SJ: So as a nonboarder[1], your tuition[2] here is the same as mine . . . we'll make it a nice round number and say thirty-six thousand dollars per year. Our parents pay on a semester basis, which means that in seven semesters, yours have invested . . . Who has a calculator?

5 Justyce: A hundred and twenty-six thousand dollars.

Manny: Damn!

Doc: [*Cuts*[3] *Manny a warning look.*]

Manny: My bad[4], Doc.

SJ: For that insane[5] sum of money, we're getting the best of the best of the
10 best. Tuition includes laptops, tablets, and access to more scholarly[6] databases than most colleges have; we've got the most current editions of all college-level textbooks; our library is like . . . I can't even tell you; we have test prep courses[7] built into our curriculum from the moment we start ninth grade; and I'm pretty sure something like ninety-seven percent of the
15 teachers at this school are PhDs, right, Doc?

Doc: Something like that.

SJ: You wouldn't expect anything less based on the amount of money you're paying, right?

Jared: Do you have a point here?

20 SJ: I do. Now say you have a black guy—not Justyce, but someone else— whose single parent's income falls beneath the poverty line[8]. He lives in a really crummy[9] area and goes to a public school that has fifteen-year-old textbooks and no computers. Most of the teachers are fresh out of college and leave after a year. Some psychological testing has been done at this

---

1 nonboarder: student who doesn't live at school **2** tuition [tuˈɪʃn]: money that you pay to go to university **3** cut sb. a look (infml): look at sb. quickly
4 my bad (infml): I made a mistake. **5** insane: extremely high **6** scholarly [ˈskɑːlərli]: referring to academic study **7** prep (n): (here) preparation **8** poverty line: level of income needed to pay the basic things you need **9** crummy (infml): very bad quality

school, and the majority of students there, this guy included, are found to suffer from low self-esteem[1] and struggle with standardized testing because of stereotype threat[2]—basically, the guy knows people expect him to underperform[3], which triggers severe test anxiety[4] that causes him to underperform.   5

Doc: [*Grins.*]

SJ: Now erase the two backgrounds. We'll keep it simple and say GPA-wise[5], you have a four-point-oh and he has a three-point-six. Test scores, you got a fifteen-eighty, right? Well, this guy got an eleven-twenty. Based on GPA and scores only, which one of you is more likely to get into a good college?   10

Jared: Me. Obviously.

SJ: Is that fair? You've had access to WAY more than he has . . . would it be fair for a college to consider only GPA and test scores in determining who deserves to get in?

Jared: It's not my fault my parents can afford to send me to a good school—   15

Justyce: Is it his fault his mom can't, man?

Everyone: [. . .]

SJ: I'm not saying the system is perfect. Yes, people who legitimately[6] aren't as qualified get picked[7] over people who are, and yes, it's usually people of

---

1 self-esteem: feeling about yourself **2** stereotype threat: psychological term that describes a self-confirming belief that one may be evaluated based on a negative stereotype about one's racial, ethnic, gender, or cultural group. Researchers Claude Steele and Joshua Aronson did experiments that showed that Black college students performed worse on standardized tests than their white peers when they were reminded, before taking the tests, that their racial group tends to do poorly on such exams. When their race was not mentioned, however, Black students performed similarly to their white peers. *Bedrohung durch Stereotype* **3** underperform: not be as successful as expected **4** anxiety (about/over sth.) [æŋ'zaɪəti]: feeling of nervousness or worry (about/over sth.)
5 GPA (grade point average) (AE): measure of academic achievement
6 legitimate [lɪ'dʒɪtɪmət]: rightful, for a fair reason **7** pick (v): choose

color getting picked over white people. But before you say something "isn't fair," you should consider your starting point versus someone else's.

Jared: Whatever. All I know is that no matter what college I end up at, when I see a minority, I'm gonna wonder if they're qualified to be there.

5 Everyone: [. . .]

Justyce: Damn, it's like that, Jared?

Jared: I mean . . . wait, that didn't come out right—

SJ: And there you have it, folks.

Everyone: [. . .]

December 13

DEAR MARTIN,

Can you explain why everywhere I turn, I run into people who wanna keep me down[1]?

Tonight I went home because I decided to share the Yale news with Mama in person, and while she was ecstatic, what I faced[2] when I left the house brought me back as low as the "affirmative action is bullshit" discussion from class today.

Basically, when I rounded[3] the corner to head to my bus stop, Trey and a bunch of the Black Jihad dudes (the white guy included) were standing there "shootin' the sh*t,"[4] as my granddaddy used to say. When Trey asked me what the f%#k I was so happy about, I actually told them about Yale.

Yeah, I was trippin', Martin.

Trey's response? "You'll be back, smart guy. Once you see them white folks don't want yo[5] black ass at they table. They not down with[6] you bein' their equal, dawg. We'll see you soon." He grinned.

I think if the Socio Evo discussion had taken place on a different day, I could've ignored Trey. I mean what the heck does he know? I'm not even sure he's still in school, and the only white person he interacts with was standing there with his blond hair in cornrows and a gold grill that spelled out "BRAD" across his teeth.

Jared and Trey taken together, though? The whole return trip to campus, their words played catch[7] with my confidence.

Jared's test score thing really bugged me. All this talk about how "equal" things are, yet he assumed I didn't do as well as he did? And

---

1 keep sb. down: not allowing sb. to get power and status **2** face sth. (v): experience sth., have a problem, challenge in front of you **3** round sth. (v): go around
4 shoot the shit (infml): hang out with friends **5** yo (infml) (AE): your
6 be down with sth. (infml) (AE): accept sth. **7** play catch: (here) affect sth. in a negative way

NOBODY can tell me he didn't make that assumption because he's white and I'm black, Martin.

And then Trey . . . WHY does this guy insist on trying to keep me down? On the real, he's just as bad as Jared!

5 It's like I'm trying to climb a mountain, but I've got one fool trying to shove me down so I won't be on his level, and another fool tugging at my leg, trying to pull me to the ground he refuses to leave. Jared and Trey are only two people, but after today, I know that when I head to Yale next fall (because I AM going there), I'm gonna be paranoid about
10 people looking at me and wondering if I'm qualified to be there.

How do I work against this, Martin? Getting real with you, I feel a little defeated. Knowing there are people who don't want me to succeed is depressing. Especially coming from two directions.

I'm working hard to choose the moral high road like you would, but
15 it'll take more than that, won't it? Where'd you get the courage to keep climbing in the face of stuff like this? Because I know you got it from both sides.

I'm gonna try and sleep now. Get my head reset on my shoulders. Feel free to pop up in my dreams or something. Tell me what to do. Like
20 Babe Ruth did to Benny in The Sandlot (I love that movie, Martin).

—Justyce

P.S. Totally unrelated, but you know anything about love triangles? I feel like a jerk because there SJ was, cheering me forward, while Melo—as usual, only thinking of herself—wanted to hold me back. And what did I
25 do? Capitulated to the booty (and, okay, the fear of what my mama will say if I fail to keep SJ at the furthest end of the friend zone).

I've got absolutely nothing on this one. How did I even end up in this position? I'm a decent-lookin' dude, but TWO gorgeous girls wanting the J-Mac?

30 I can't even handle it, Martin.

CHAPTER 8

Before Justyce's butt has a chance to sink into the leather of the Riverses'[1] basement couch, Manny's already talking crazy. "So how long you plan to hold out[2] on ya boy?" He doesn't turn away from the movie he's watching on mute[3] while an old Deuce Diggs track thumps[4] through the speakers. 5

"I won't even pretend to know what you're talking about," Jus replies. "Yo, what album is this? I don't think I've heard this cut[5] before."

"Mixtape from a few years ago. Don't change the subject."

Jus looks at Manny. "What subject?" 10

"Dawg, who just dropped you off[6]?" Manny says.

"SJ. Which you know from the *I'll have SJ drop me off* text message you responded to fifteen minutes ago."

"Exaaaaactly."

"Exactly what?" 15

"You and SJ."

"What about me and SJ?"

Manny stares at Jus like he just said *Two plus two is five*.

"*What*, Manny?"

Manny shakes his head. "I thought we were boys, Jus." 20

"Whatever. Turn the TV up." Justyce tucks his hands behind his head.

"Just tell me how long."

"How long *WHAT*, fool?"

---

1 Riverses': belonging to the Rivers family **2** hold out on sth.: not tell sb. some new or important information **3** on mute: with the sound turned off **4** thump (v): make a loud sound **5** cut (n): (here) version **6** drop sb. off: drive sb. to a place

"How long you been hookin' up[1] with SJ, man! Why you over here playing dumb[2]?"

Jus rolls his eyes. "I'm not hookin' up with SJ, Manny."

"Everybody knows, man."

5 "Everybody knows *what*?"

"That you're over at her house *every damn day.* You know Jessa Northup is her neighbor. She told us. Says SJ's parents are obsessed[3] with you. Call you Jusmeister and shit."

Jus drags his hands down his face. He knew Jessa was nosy[4], but 10 damn. "First of all, you sound like a damn girl right now with all this gossiping[5] shit. Second, I'm *not* over there every day. Third, when I *am* there, it's for debate stuff. And fourth, Mr. and Mrs. F liking me is irrelevant[6]."

Manny rolls his eyes. "So all you go over there for is debate?"

15 "*Yes,* Manny. The state tournament is in three and a half weeks."

"Okay . . . and that's all y'all *ever* talk about?"

Justyce's brow[7] furrows[8]. "I mean, we occasionally talk about other stuff but—"

"SEE! It's something going on between y'all, man! I can see that 20 shit all over you!"

Justyce shakes his head and settles down into the couch. "I'm not talking about this anymore. You gonna turn the movie up, or what?"

"Jus, I'm your best friend!"

"Dawg." Justyce sits up. Turns to look Manny in the eye. "I'm only 25 gonna say this once, so listen closely, all right? There is *nothing* going on between me and SJ."

Manny stares right back. "Jus, I *know* you like her, man. And she obviously likes you—"

"Doesn't matter." Justyce sinks back into the leather.

---

1 hook up with sb.: meet sb. and spend time, have a sexual relationship
2 play dumb: act stupid when you are not, act like you do not know sth.
3 be obsessed with sb./sth.: always thinking about sb./sth. and unable to think about sb./sth. else **4** nosy: curious, too interested **5** gossip (v): talk about others
6 irrelevant: not important **7** brow: forehead **8** furrow (v): pull your eyebrows together when you are worried/concentrating

"It *does,* though—"

"No, it doesn't."

"You trippin'[1], man. SJ's a gorgeous girl AND she's perfect for you."

"Drop it."

"Come on, Jus—"   5

"I said it doesn't matter, Manny!"

"Why *not*?"

Justyce takes a deep breath. "Manny, my mama would blow every gasket[2] in a fifty-mile radius."

"Huh?"   10

"SJ is white."

Manny draws back, puts his hand over his heart, and mock-gasps[3]. "*What?* You're kidding me."

"Shut up, fool."

"Whatever." Manny waves him off. "She's not *white* white. She's   15
Jewish. It's different."

Jus sighs.

"They were slaves too, dawg. And then the Holocaust. Even now—"

"I know what you mean. Won't matter to my mama, though. SJ's   20
skin is white."

Manny doesn't respond.

"My mama is not down with that."

Still no response.

Justyce exhales.   25

"No offense, Jus, but that might be the dumbest thing I've ever heard," Manny finally says.

Jus shrugs. "Is what it is. And since pissing my mama off[4] ain't real high on my to-do list, SJ and I are *strictly* friends. Besides, me and Mel are talkin' again."   30

---

1 trip (v): (here) be completely wrong because you are not thinking properly
2 blow a gasket (infml): become very angry **3** mock-gasp: pretend to be shocked
or surprised **4** piss sb. off (infml): make sb. very angry

Manny smacks his forehead. "I was wrong before," he says. "*THAT* is the dumbest thing I've ever heard."

"Shut up, man."

"Jus, if Melo and SJ are diverging[1] paths on the road of life, you're
5　headed for a dead end[2], my friend."

"Where do you *get* this shit, Manny?"

"I'm just sayin'. Mama aside, you're making the wrong decision."

Jus snorts. "No offense, but I refuse to take relationship advice from a dude who's never been in one."

10　"Whoa[3] now! Just cuz[4] I don't want a serious girlfriend at the moment doesn't mean I don't know what it takes to maintain[5] a relationship."

"Ah, here we go."

"I'm serious, Jus. You think I've learned *nothing* from watching
15　my parents over the last seventeen and a half years?"

"Whatever, man. Can we *please* drop this?"

They fall into a weighty[6] silence, both staring at the massive television screen but neither actually watching the movie.

Out of nowhere, Manny says, "You know I've got the opposite
20　problem, right?"

"What?"

"I'ma[7] tell you something, but don't laugh at me, all right? I'm trusting you with a deep, dark secret."

Jus lifts an eyebrow.

25　Manny inhales, filling his cheeks with air before blowing it out. "I'm scared of black girls, man."

"Huh?"

"Black girls. I've never really encountered[8] a nonfamily one."

"Okay . . ."

---

1 diverge [daɪˈvɜːrdʒ]: go in different directions **2** dead end: street that is closed at one end **3** whoa [wəʊ]: sound to make a horse stop or slow down **4** cuz (infml): because **5** maintain sth.: keep or continue sth. **6** weighty: serious **7** I'ma (infml): I am going to **8** encounter sb.: meet sb.

"There are none in our grade. The only ones I know are my cousins and they're . . . a lot."

"A lot?"

"Like real *attitude-y*[1] and kinda . . ." Manny swallows. "Ghetto[2]."

Justyce doesn't know what to say. It's not like he has any experience in this area either. Melo's half black, but she's def not the type of girl Manny's talking about.

Manny goes on: "I know that's a stereotype or whatever, but I've literally never experienced anything else. My folks are all excited about me going to Morehouse[3] next year, but I'm nervous as hell."

"How come?"

"You're my *only* black friend, dawg. I'm supposed to go from this all-white world to an all-black one overnight?"

Jus doesn't respond.

"Anyway. My bad for just laying all that on you."

Jus shrugs. "It's cool."

"I should've applied to Princeton[4] or somethin'. Woulda been more familiar." Manny sighs.

Jus shakes Manny's shoulder. "You'll be fine, man. I'm *sure* there'll be plenty of dudes you'll vibe[5] with at Morehouse just like you vibe with me."

"It's Spelman[6] I'm really worried about. You know it's right next door. Black girls *everywhere*."

Jus laughs.

"And you know I love women, man. What if I get there and *none* of them are feelin' me?"

"I wish I knew what to tell you, Manny. All I can say is they're not all alike, just like we aren't."

---

1 -y: full of, having the characteristics of **2** ghetto (infml) (AE): relating to being from a minority area and a lower/poorer social status **3** Morehouse, Princeton, Spelman: US colleges/universities **4** Morehouse, Princeton, Spelman: US colleges/universities **5** vibe with: get along with **6** Morehouse, Princeton, Spelman: US colleges/universities

Manny nods. "Touché[1], my dawg."

They lapse[2] into silence again.

Then: "Jus, I'ma say this last thing, then I'll get outta your business."

5   "Oh boy. Here we go."

"I get wanting to please your mom. The only reason I'm even *going* to Morehouse is because it's been my 'SpelHouse' alumni parents' dream for me since they found out I was a boy. But passing up on a good thing because your mom wouldn't approve . . . I don't
10 know about that, man. Especially when it comes to something as stupid as race."

Justyce snorts.

"You're still doing that MLK thing, right? What would *he* do?"

"I wouldn't know considering Ms. Coretta[3] was black."

15 "Shut up. You know what I mean. If you're doing this Be Like Martin thing, do it for real. Refusing to date a girl because she's white is probably *not* the Kingly[4] way, bruh."

Justyce glares at Manny. "I knew I shouldn't've told your punk ass anything."

20 Manny smirks and grabs the TV remote from the ottoman. Then he slouches[5] down into the couch and unmutes the movie.

---

1 touché [tu:ˈʃeɪ]: expression to admit that another person has had the better argument **2** lapse into silence: stop talking or being active **3** Ms Coretta: Coretta Scott King (April 27, 1927 – January 30, 2006), American civil rights leader and author who was married to Martin Luther King Jr. **4** Kingly way: the way Martin Luther king would have done it **5** slouch (v): move in a lazy way

CHAPTER 9

Justyce is so focused on the upcoming state debate tournament, he barely notices Christmas and New Year's as they blow by[1].

Of course, the morning of the tournament itself, it's the last thing on his mind.

For one thing, two nights ago, he broke up with Melo again, he's pretty sure for the last time. As they sat in her basement with her rambling[2] about stuff that has no bearing[3] on anything that *matters,* Manny's words rang through Jus's head like a five-bell[4] alarm: *If Melo and SJ are diverging paths on the road of life, you're headed for a dead end.*

Speaking of SJ, that's the other reason he can't focus. As she steps out of the hotel elevator, smiling at him like he made the sun rise, his brain goes to mush[5]. Though they cleared things up the day after the Melo/SJ cafeteria showdown—Jus: "I'm sorry for sidelining[6] you, S." SJ: "I forgive you, jackass[7]. Don't let it happen again."—seeing SJ now, Justyce can tell how big of an idiot he's been. Especially considering the fitted[8] skirt-suit[9] and heels[10] she's rockin'[11].

"You ready?" she says once she's standing right in front of him.

He just stares.

Her smile fades and she touches her cheek. "What? Is there something on my face?"

"No." Justyce clears his throat. "You look really nice is all."

---

1 blow by: happen or pass quickly **2** ramble (v): talk about sth. in a confused way **3** bearing on sth. (n): connection with sth., relevance to sth. **4** five-bell alarm: very loud noise **5** mush (n): any soft, thick mass **6** sideline sb.: make sb. seem not included in what people are doing **7** jackass: stupid person **8** fitted: made to follow the body shape **9** skirt-suit: uniform with a skirt **10** heels: shoes with a raised part at the back **11** rock (v): (here) wear

"Oh. Thanks." Her cheeks turn pink. Justyce thinks he might combust[1]. She winks and tugs at his tie, which matches the deep maroon[2] of her suit, just like they planned. "You're not too bad yourself."

5 Just then Doc comes around the corner from the breakfast buffet with the rest of the team in tow[3]. "Good morning, my little lion cubs[4]!" He steps between Justyce and SJ and drapes an arm around each of their shoulders. "Ready to rumble[5]?"

"You bet your ass we are—"

10 "Watch it, Ms. Friedman," Jus says in Doc's voice.

Doc and SJ laugh. "Seriously, though," Doc says. "I know your round isn't until after lunch, but you feel like you're *ready* ready?"

What Doc isn't saying: he still hasn't gotten his mind around the fact that his top two debaters elected to forgo[6] the actual *debate* 15 rounds of the tournament and focus solely[7] on advanced pairs argumentation.

In other words, they've got one shot[8].

"We're as ready as we'll ever be," SJ says. She reaches past Doc to squeeze Jus's hand.

20 Jus looks at her, and she smiles.

He has no clue how he's gonna get through this day.

Truth be told[9], Jus and SJ hadn't settled[10] on a topic until a couple of weeks ago. They were in her basement. She was sitting cross-legged with her laptop open in this massive wicker chair[11] Mr. F imported 25 from Israel, and Jus was pacing[12] around the pool table, using the cue[13] like a hobbit staff[14], trying not to ogle[15] her legs.

---

1 combust: start burning **2** maroon: dark red-brown **3** in tow (infml): following closely **4** cub: young animal **5** rumble (v): fight against sb. else **6** forgo: give up, do without **7** sole [səʊl] (adj): only **8** shot (n): try, chance **9** truth be told: being honest **10** settle on: decide on **11** wicker chair: *Korbstuhl* **12** pace around: walk up and down **13** cue [kjuː] (n): wooden stick for hitting the ball in pool or billiards **14** staff (n): long stick used for walking **15** ogle ['əʊgl] (v): look at sb. showing sexual interest

He sighed as he passed her again. "Maybe we should just do the stereotype threat thing. We've got a solid argument there."

"Yeah, minus the fact that the guy presenting it wasn't affected at all." She smirked.

"Well, we gotta pick somethin', S," he said. "Like now. We're run- 5 nin' out of time—"

"I know, I know. Give me a sec, okay? I'm working on something."

She went back to typing, and Jus's mind went in a different direction. Over the past couple of days, it'd really sunk[1] in that this would be his and SJ's final tournament together. When it was over, his 10 excuse for hanging out with her would be kaput[2].

And then what would he do?

He glanced over at her again. She was rockin' her glasses with her hair in a messy knot. His favorite way for her to be. Yeah, just last night he'd been at Melo's—and definitely not for anything aca- 15 demic—but being around SJ was just . . . different. He didn't wanna let it go but had no clue how to keep it going.

"Oh my god!"

"What?"

"I think I've got it! C'mere[3]!" She uncrossed her legs and made 20 room for him in the chair.

As he squeezed in beside her and felt her whole left side pressed against his right, he had to take a clandestine[4] deep breath—she smelled like fruit and flowers—and force himself to focus.

"So check this out," she said, rotating[5] the screen so he could see it. 25 "The Myth of the Superpredator[6]" was the title of the article. "The gist of this: back in the nineties, some big-shot researchers predicted that the number of violent crimes committed by African American teen

---

1 sink in: be fully understood and realized **2** kaput (adj): useless **3** c'mere (infml): come here **4** clandestine [klænˈdestɪn] (adj): done secretly **5** rotate: turn around **6** superpredator [ˈsuːpərpredətər] (n): sb. who attacks others without mercy

males would skyrocket[1] in the years to follow. The 'leading authority' on the matter dubbed[2] these potential criminals superpredators."

Justyce already knew about the superpredator myth—he'd stumbled upon the whole thing while trying to deal with his own
5 profiling[3] trauma[4]. But he let SJ keep going because when would he get to see her all absorbed in debate research and talking a million miles per minute again? He'd miss this.

"Fortunately, the prediction was incorrect," she went on. "Crime rates among youth plummeted[5]."

10 He smiled. "Okay . . ."

"*Un*fortunately, it seems the fear of young black guys created by this research is alive and well." She ran a fingertip over his wrist.

Annnnd time to get up.

He went back to pacing. "So where would we go with this, S?"

15 "Well, I'm thinking we could do an argument on racial profiling."

Jus stopped. "You're not serious."

"I am."

"So you've lost[6] it, is what you're really telling me."

"Oh come on. What do we have to lose?"

20 "Uhh, the tournament?"

"Screw[7] the tournament." She shut her laptop and came over to where he was. "This is something people need to hear about, Jus. It's an argumentation gold mine!"

"Mmmm . . ." It wasn't that he didn't believe they could form a
25 solid[8] argument—she was right: the numbers spoke for themselves.

The real issue? He didn't wanna be the black guy accused of "playing the race card[9]" at a state tournament.

---

1 skyrocket (v): increase quickly 2 dub (v): give sth. a nickname or label
3 profiling: act of predicting sb.'s behaviour based on a specific characteristic
e.g. race 4 trauma: shocking experience that may lead to mental illness
5 plummet (v): fall down straight and at high speed 6 lose it: be out of your
mind 7 screw sb./sth. (sl): an offensive way of showing you do not care about
sb./sth. 8 solid (adj): well-built and stable 9 play the race card: using the issue
of your race to your advantage

He turned to her then. Though he prolly shouldn't have. Cuz *feel-ings.* "I don't know about this, S."

"I didn't sleep for a week after what happened to you, Jus," she said. "I know we might be throwing away our chance at a win, but if we can get some facts out there, maybe make people *think* a little ₅ bit, it'll be worth it, right?"

Jus didn't say a word.

She threw an arm over his shoulders. Boob[1] on the biceps. "It's our last hurrah," she said. "Let's go out with a bang[2]."

"S, I—" ₁₀

"Come onnnnnn, Jussy!"

She pouted[3].

He sighed. There would be no turning her down[4].

"Fine," he said. "Let's do it."

Because of their combined debate record for the season—eight ₁₅ wins, one loss, one tie[5]—Justyce and SJ are the final pair in their division[6] to present their argument. When their names are called, they step into the glaring stage lights and up to the adjacent[7] podiums. The only people Jus can see are the three judges.

The center judge says *You may begin,* and SJ launches[8] into their ₂₀ introduction. With her final sentence—"We are here to argue that racial disparities[9] in the US criminal justice system are largely due to racial profiling"—a murmur[10] trickles through the audience. Jus's stomach clenches, and a bead of sweat runs down his side from his

---

1 boob (n) (infml.): breast **2** with a bang: excitingly, impressively **3** pout (v): pushing your bottom lip forward to playfully show your irritation **4** turn sb./sth. down: say no to sb./sth. (e.g. an invitation, request) **5** tie (n): result of a team competition where both teams have the same score **6** division: teams that are grouped together to compete against each other **7** adjacent [ə'dʒeɪsnt]: next to each other **8** launch into sth.: begin sth. immediately **9** racial disparity: unfair and prejudiced treatment of racial groups **10** murmur (n): sound made by people talking quietly to each other

armpit. Two of the judges are stone-faced[1], but when he locks eyes[2] with the third—a white lady—she nods at him.

His eyes shift among the three of them as he and SJ rattle[3] off the statistics that support their argument: drug use versus drug
5 conviction[4] numbers, arrest numbers in minority-populated versus white-populated police zones . . . By the time they get to the super-predator stuff, all three judges are rapt[5]. That's when Jus realizes SJ was right: whether or not they win this tournament, he *needed* to talk about this in a public forum.

10 When they're done, Jus feels like he's walking in a dream. He and SJ get backstage, and the team sweeps[6] them up in hugs and high fives. Doc, with visibly moist[7] eyeballs, tells Jus how proud he is, and a black guy from another team nods at him from across the room. Some random cute girl from another school brings him water with
15 her number scrawled[8] on the cup, and he sees SJ slip it in the gar-bage when she thinks he's not looking.

He has no clue how much time passes between them leaving the stage and hearing the emcee[9] return to announce the results, but the next thing he knows, Doc and the team are filing out to return
20 to their seats.

None of it feels real.

Without thinking too much about it, he drapes an arm around SJ's shoulders. She turns to wrap her arms around his torso[10], and when she buries her face in his neck, his other arm slips around her
25 waist.

They breathe.

---

1 stone-faced: not showing any emotions **2** lock eyes with sb.: look each other in the eyes **3** rattle off: say sth. fast and without any effort **4** conviction: when sb. is officially declared to be guilty of a crime **5** rapt: being fascinated and absorbed by sth. **6** sweep sb. up: lift sb. up quickly and smoothly **7** moist: wet **8** scrawl (v) [skrɔːl]: write untidily (making it difficult to read) **9** emcee (n) [emˈsiː]: host or presenter of an event **10** torso: stomach and chest part of the body

The emcee calls third place. It's not them. SJ inhales, and Jus feels her ribs expand[1]. When the emcee calls second and it's not them, Jus squeezes tighter. "S, I just wanna sa—"

"Hush it. You can tell me later."

"Bossy."   5

She chuckles[2]. It makes him feel better than he's felt in a long time.

"And your state champions in the advanced pairs argumentation division: from Braselton Preparatory Academy, Justyce McAllister and Sarah-Jane Friedman!"   10

They don't let go.

---

1 expand (v): (here) move outwards   **2** chuckle (v): laugh (quietly)

January 13

Martin, I think I'm losing it.

I've avoided writing to you about this because it really doesn't have any bearing on the Be Like Martin experiment. Then again, I guess it
5 could be considered a failed attempt at "romantic integration" or something . . . Anyway, after the dream I just had—which I definitely won't put in here because it's not appropriate—I gotta get some stuff off my chest[1].

So SJ and I won our division of the state debate tournament. When
10 we returned backstage after receiving our medals, everything felt different. I couldn't stop thinking about the way we were hugging just before they announced all the winners, so when she turned to face me looking all beautiful, I knew that was it. No more resisting.

We're standing there grinning at each other, so I looked at her lips
15 and leaned in for the kill[2] . . .

AND SHE TURNED AWAY! Just straight-up rotated[3] 180 degrees and started walking in the opposite direction! "You see Doc anywhere?" she said over her shoulder.

That girl KNEW I was about to kiss her, Martin!

20 She avoided me for the rest of the night, and then wouldn't talk to me on the ride back to school in her car Sunday morning. Just cranked up the music like I wasn't even there.

THEN, when we got to the dorms, and I reached for the car door handle, she goes, "So congrats again on winning the tournament." (Like
25 she didn't just win it with me?) "Working with you has been a real pleasure[4], and I know you'll do great at Yale. See you around, Justyce!"

It took me a minute to get the hint and exit because I was trying to figure out the identity of this alien cyborg and what the hell it did with my debate partner/good friend/girl-I-really-wanted-to-kiss named SJ.

---

1 get sth. off your chest: talk about sth. that has made you sad **2** lean in for the kill: lean towards sb. to kiss them **3** rotate: move or turn around **4** pleasure (n): sth. that makes you feel happy

As soon as I grabbed my stuff and shut the door, she drove off. Just like that.

I was ready to go against my mama for this girl, Martin!

I don't know what happened. I thought things were going well! I swear since Manny called me out for not being like you, SJ and I have been tighter than ever. The chemistry was off the charts[1] . . . I know I didn't read the signals wrong, did I?

I have no idea what to do now. I can't eat. Can barely sleep. Can't stay focused . . . Everywhere I turn, there's a reminder of this girl. Can't pass a brunette[2] without doing a double take[3]. Manny's been on this Carrie Underwood[4] kick[5], which is what SJ liked to play in the background when we were working on debate stuff at her house.

I even went to sleep at home last night thinking being around my mama would help, but when I got there, she was watchin' Judge Judy[6]! (SJ swears she and Judge Judy are related.)

I guess I should let it go, right? I can't force her to talk to me if she doesn't want to . . .

It makes me feel wack[7] as hell, but in my mind I keep seeing the shrinking[8] taillights[9] of her car as she drove away.

Whatever. I give up.

Gonna try to sleep again now.

—J

---

1 off the charts: unexpectedly great **2** brunette [bruːˈnet] (n): woman with dark brown hair **3** do a double take: look twice at sth./sb. to make sure you really saw/recognized it/them correctly **4** Carrie Underwood: US country singer (born 1983), won the 4th season of American Idol in 2005 **5** kick (n) (infml): phase when you like sth. a lot **6** Judge Judy: popular US TV reality-based court show **7** wack (adj) (infml): crazy, bad **8** shrink (v): become smaller **9** taillights: red lights at the rear of a car

CHAPTER 10

But Justyce doesn't sleep. Not that night, nor the rest of the week.

And it's not just SJ.

A couple of mornings after she gives him the cold shoulder[1], he and the rest of the nation learn that Tavarrius Jenkins, a sixteen-year-old black kid shot by police while trying to help an older white woman in a Lexus, has died from his injuries.

On Friday after school, Jus walks into Doc's classroom wanting to talk about it and finds he's been beat to the punch[2]: SJ's in there crying her eyes out. As much as he wants to turn on his heel and jet[3], he can't seem to move.

Seeing her there—even as a friend—broken the way she is makes Justyce feel as helpless as he did the night he got arrested. Based on the way she's scowling at him, Jus can't help but wonder if he's partially to blame for her tears.

But how could he be? Didn't she turn her back on him? After they've stared each other down for forever, it feels, she wipes her face, grabs her stuff, and heads to the door. When Doc calls after her and she doesn't respond before breezing out, he turns to Justyce. "What's that all about?"

"Oh, you don't know?" Justyce says, ready to turn and leave himself. He drops down into a desk instead.

Doc crosses his arms and furrows his eyebrows. "Can't say I do, Jus."

"That's too bad, then," Justyce says, looking Doc right in the eye. "I was hoping you could tell *me*."

---

1 give sb. the cold shoulder: be unfriendly to sb. on purpose **2** beat sb. to the punch: do sth. before sb. else does it **3** turn on your heel and jet: run away from a situation as fast as possible

Needless to say[1], Jus doesn't feel like talking anymore. As soon as he thinks enough time has passed for SJ to get off campus, he says goodbye to a stupefied[2] Doc and heads to his dorm room.

He's just managed to doze[3] off when there's a knock at his door, snatching him back into consciousness[4].

"Who is it?"

"Open the door, fool."

Manny.

Jus forces himself out of bed and to the door. "What, dawg?" he says as he opens it.

"Hey, bruh, chill with all that attitude." Manny pushes past him and into the room, bringing his post–basketball practice BO[5] with him. "You sleepin' or somethin?"

"Obviously not if I'm standin' here talking to your stank[6] ass. You need a shower."

"Shut up. It's Friday night and we got places to be. Put some clothes on and let's go."

Jus returns to the bed. "Sorry, dawg. I don't really feel like goin' nowhere tonight."

"That wasn't a request, Jus. Don't think I haven't noticed how mopey[7] you been this week. Being alone in your current state isn't good for your mental health, man. Blake's birthday party is tonight, and you're coming with me."

"No. I'm not."

"All right, then." Manny pulls Jus's desk chair over to the bed and sits down. "You wanna stay in bed? Cool. My dirty ass will be right here with you."

"Aww, come on, Manny! Get outta here with that." Jus pulls a pillow over his nose.

---

1 needless to say: it is clearly true **2** stupefy (v): surprise or shock sb. so that they unable to think clearly **3** doze off: fall asleep **4** consciousness: state in which you are not asleep **5** BO (body odor): bad smell from an unwashed human body **6** stank (sl): very stinky **7** mopey: depressed

Manny kicks his shoes off and tucks his hands behind his head, unleashing[1] the full force of his funk into the room. He smirks.

Jus really can't stand this guy sometimes.

He takes a deep breath . . . which is a bad idea. "*Damn*, you stink,
5 dawg. Fine, I'll go."

"Great!" Manny hops up. "I'ma go get my car from the lot. I'll meet you downstairs in ten."

"Yeah, all right."

"You won't regret it, man." Manny walks out and leaves the door
10 open.

Justyce really isn't in the best headspace[2] to be accepting the "pregame beverage[3]" that gets shoved into his hand once they get to Manny's basement. He'd never say it aloud, but Jus would much rather be at SJ's watching National Geographic[4] than here waiting
15 for Manny to get ready. Just thinking about her is making him crazy. Before he knows it, his cup is empty and he's reaching for the flask Manny left on the ottoman.

"Dawg, you *cryin'*?" Manny says when he finally emerges from his room smelling like he bathed in Armani Code[5].

20 "Naw[6], bruh, I'm good." Jus wipes his face on his sleeve. "Got something in my eye."

Manny sits down. "All this about SJ?"

"Huh?"

"I heard what happened at the tournament."

25 He can't be serious. "What'd you hear?"

"That you tried to kiss her and she cold-shouldered your ass."

Jus shakes his head. "How could you *possibly* have heard that?"

"Small school." Manny shrugs. "People talk."

Jus doesn't reply.

---

1 unleash sth. on/upon sb./sth. [ʌnˈliːʃ]: release, let go **2** headspace: state of mind **3** pregame beverage (sl): alcoholic drink that you have on a way to a party **4** National Geographic: popular TV channel that features documentaries on nature, science and history **5** Armani Code: heavy perfume for men **6** naw (sl): no

"You were in love with her, huh? Heart's all broken and shit?"

"Whoa now, dawg. Slow down with all *that.*"

"Jus, you're sittin' here *crying* abou—"

"I'm not cryin', Manny."

"Whatever, fool." Manny slouches down and stares up at the ceiling. "That's *gotta* be love." 5

For a minute, they sit in silence, Manny doing whatever he's doing and Jus trying to keep images of SJ out of his head. He switches gears to the other thing on his mind: "You hear about Tavarrius Jenkins?"

"The kid who got shot in Florida, right?" 10

"Yeah. He died yesterday."

"Damn. That's sad."

"I keep thinkin' that coulda been me. What if that cop thought I had a gun?"

"You didn't, though." 15

"Neither did Tavarrius," Jus says, feeling the anger build. "That's exactly what I'm sayin'. Guy's walking down the street with his boys and stops to help a lady who ran out of gas on the wrong side of town. Cops get there and tell him to put his hands up cuz they think he's robbing her, and when he does, they open fire cuz they think his 20 cell phone is a gun. Shit's fucked up, man." Jus grabs the flask again and takes a swig[1]. "Niggas gettin' shot for carrying candy and cell phones and shit. Can you imagine what woulda happened to *me* if I'd had *my* cell phone out that night? I could be dead, dawg. And for what?" He swigs again just to feel the burn. 25

"Aiight, that's enough." Manny takes the flask back and pats Jus's knee. "Let's hit B's party. You obviously need the distraction."

Part of Justyce wants to shake Manny. Ask why he cares more about some stupid white-boy party than he does about the unjust death of a guy who looks like him. 30

Too bad he doesn't have it left in him[2].

"Yeah, all right," he says. "Let's go."

---

1 take a swig: take another sip **2** have it left in sb.: still have the power to stand up for yourself

Perhaps if Justyce hadn't downed[1] half the liquid in Manny's refilled[2] flask on the way to Blake's house, the wooden lawn jockeys[3] with black skin and big red lips standing guard[4] at the bottom of Blake's porch[5] steps wouldn't bother him so much. There's a good chance
5 that if he'd "slowed down" when Manny told him to, he wouldn't feel fury[6] when he sees that the wall behind the bar in Blake's basement is lined[7] with posters from "William H. West's[8] Big Minstrel Jubilee."

But Justyce didn't slow down. He kept drinking until Manny literally took the flask from his hand and slipped it into the driver-side
10 door where Jus couldn't reach it. So when the birthday boy comes running up to Manny and Justyce, Jus is ready to blow.

Manny: Happy birthday, man!

Jus: Yeah, happy birthday.

Blake: Bros! *So* glad y'all made it!

15 Manny smiles and winks at Justyce like *Told you.*

"Yo, listen," Blake goes on. He's definitely been drinking too. "There's this *fine*-ass[9] black girl here from Decatur Prep, and I was thinking you guys could wingman[10] it up for me and shit. Home-girl's[11] got the fattest ass I've ever *seen,* and I think if she meets my
20 niggas, I'll have a good chance of getting' her upstairs. You feel me, dogs?" He nudges Jus and grins.

Manny's smile collapses[12]. He looks over at Justyce. Almost like he *knows* everything's about to go to hell.

"Is this fool serious right now?" Jus says.

25 Blake looks confused.

"Jus, chill," Manny says.

---

1 down sth. (infml): drink sth. quickly **2** refilled: filled up again **3** lawn jockey: Statue in Form eines Reiters beim Pferderennen für den Garten **4** stand guard: protect sth. **5** porch [pɔːrtʃ]: covered section to an entrance **6** fury: rage, anger **7** be lined with sth.: be covered with sth. **8** William H. West (1853-1902): white American who produced a band of white entertainers (minstrel) that performed with blackened faces **9** -ass (sl): added to an adjective to make its meaning stronger **10** wingman sth. up (infml): supporting another man usu. in getting to know a woman **11** homegirl (sl): girl from your hometown, neighborhood or similar social background **12** collapse: fall down

"Hell nah, I'm not 'bouta[1] *chill*. Ya boy's got racist lawn gnomes[2] and white people in blackface hanging on the walls, now he pulls this shit[3], and you want me to *chill*?"

Blake rolls his eyes. "Dude, none of that crap is mine. My mom's great-uncle was one of those performers, so she hung up some post- ⁵ ers. No big deal."

"You coming over here asking us to help you *use* a black girl IS a big deal, Blake. That's not to mention you tossin'[4] the n-word[5] around like you own[6] it."

Blake: You don't own it any more than I do, bro. Nobody *owns* ¹⁰ words. I'd think you'd know that as someone "smart enough" to get into Yale.

Manny: All right, y'all, let's calm down before this gets outta hand.

Justyce: It's already outta hand, Manny. Your boy Blake is a racist. ¹⁵

Blake: What is it with you people[7] and the goddamn race card, huh?

Justyce: *We* people. You realize Manny is one of us people too, right?

Blake: Except Manny's got some sense and doesn't make every- ²⁰ thing about race. Why don't you loosen[8] the hell up?

Justyce: Too bad you weren't around to say that to the cop who cuffed me for tryna to help my girl.

Blake: *Ex*-girl, you mean? Didn't she dump your ass?

At this point, Jared and Tyler walk up, both with a red cup in one ²⁵ hand and a beer in the other. "Homies!" Jared says.

It just makes Justyce madder.

Jus: Man, I'm sick of y'all acting like you got all this leeway[9].

---

1 'bouta (infml): about to **2** gnome [nəʊm]: fantastic dwarfish creature that protects treasure **3** pull shit (sl): tell lies or be offensive and disrespectful
4 toss (v): throw sth. without care **5** n-word: synonym for a racist word that was used to describe people of color **6** own sth. (v): possess sth. **7** 'you people' is a term that, in this context, is normally used by a white person when they gener-alise about or stereotype Black people **8** loosen up: relax **9** leeway: available amount of freedom to act and talk

Jared: Wow, dude. What crawled up[1] your ass?

Tyler: (*Laughs.*)

Jus: Fuck you, Jared.

Jared: Whoa, now . . .

5 Blake: Dude, don't disrespect my bros at *my* party.

Manny: Jus, let's just go.

Jus: (*Points at Blake.*) Watch your back, dawg.

Blake: Wait, are you *threatening* me?

Jared: (*Laughs.*) Better watch out, B. You know Justyce grew up in
10 the hood. He's gonna call up his gangsta homies to ride through on
your ass and bust[2] some ca—

By the time Jus is seeing colors other than red[3], his left hand and
right jaw are throbbing[4], and there's something warm running down
his chin. Jared's scrambling[5] up from the floor with a split lip and a
15 swelling[6] eye, and Blake is on his hands and knees with blood pour-
ing out of his nose and onto the carpet.

No pointed hood to stop the flow this time.

There's a set of arms around Jus, pinning *his* arms to his sides.
"Let me go," he says, twisting out of the grip of whoever's holding
20 him.

Manny. Whose lip is bleeding too.

Tyler seems to be the only one who got away unscathed[7] . . . but
then Justyce sees him shake out his right hand.

Of course a crowd has gathered.

25 Manny: What the hell is your problem, Justyce?

Jus: Man, don't even say nothing to me right now.

Manny draws back[8]. "Ex*cuse* me? Don't say nothin' to *you*?"

Jus: You're just as bad as they are.

---

1 crawl up (v): move slowly upwards, like an insect **2** bust a cap (sl): shoot a
bullet into sb. **3** see red: become angry **4** throb (v): experience pain that pulses
5 scramble up: pick yourself up from the ground in a disorderly fashion
6 swell (v): increase in size **7** unscathed [ʌnˈskeɪðd]: not being damaged or
harmed **8** draw back: take a step or move away from sth./sb.

Manny: What are you *talking* about? I don't know where all this *me against the world* shit is comin' from but you really need to check yourself[1].

Jus: These dudes disrespect you—disrespect *us*—all the time, and you never say anything about it. You just go along with what- 5 ever they say.

Manny: These are my *friends,* Jus. You're way too sensitive, man.

Jus: Lemme[2] guess: that's what they said when you took offense at some racist joke, right?

Manny: Bruh, you trippin' *hard.* You need to go cool off[3] or some- 10 thin'.

Justyce shakes his head. Looks Manny over from head to toe[4]. "You know what, Manny? You're a sellout[5]. Good luck at Morehouse next year." He shoves through the crowd and makes his way to the back door with people murmuring as he goes. Just before he pulls it 15 open, he hears, "Thanks for ruining my birthday, asshole!"

Justyce trudges[6] up the hill. Starts walking in the direction he thinks will lead him out of Blake's megamansion[7] neighborhood. He's still drunk and can't see straight, but if he can find his way back to the main road, he can find his way back to school. 20

He doesn't know how long he's been walking or how far he's gone before a navy[8] Range Rover pulls up[9] beside him.

"Get in," Manny says from inside.

"Naw, man. I'm good."

"Jus, it's thirty degrees and you're going the wrong damn way. 25 Stop being a jackass and get in the car."

"I said no, Manny."

Manny's car jerks[10] forward and suddenly whips into Justyce's path.

---

1 check yourself (sl): think again about your way of thinking/behaving
2 lemme (infml): let me **3** cool off: become calm **4** look sb. over from head to toe: inspect sb. closely **5** sellout: disloyal person **6** trudge (v): move forward with slow and heavy steps **7** megamansion [ˈmeɡəmænʃn]: extremely large house
8 navy (adj): dark blue **9** pull up: stop a vehicle in front of sth. **10** jerk (v): move suddenly and abruptly

"What the hell, man? You tryna hit me?"

"Get in the damn car, Jus!"

Justyce clenches his jaw.

"Dawg, if you care *anything* about this friendship, you will get
5   your punk ass in the car right now."

Manny looks at Jus.

Jus looks at Manny.

Manny reaches over and opens the passenger door.

Jus turns around and starts walking in the opposite direction.

January 19

DEAR MARTIN,

You know, I don't get how you did it. Just being straight up. Every day I walk through the halls of that elitist-ass[1] school, I feel like I don't belong there, and every time Jared or one of them opens their damn mouth, I'm reminded they agree. Every time I turn on the news and see another black person gunned down, I'm reminded that people look at me and see a threat[2] instead of a human being.

There was some white dude on TV after the Tavarrius Jenkins thing broke talking about how cases like his and Shemar Carson's "deflect from the issue of black-on-black crime[3]," but how are black people supposed to know how to treat each other with respect when since we were brought over here, we've been told we're not respectable?

What the hell are we supposed to do, Martin? What am I supposed to do? Be like Manny and act like there's nothing wrong with a white dude asking his "niggas" to help him exploit[4] a black girl? Do I just take what they dish out[5], try to stop being "so sensitive"? What do I do when my very identity is being mocked[6] by people who refuse to admit there's a problem?

I know I did the wrong thing tonight, but right now I can't find it in me to be remorseful[7]. Those assholes can't seem to care about being offensive[8], so why should I give a damn about being agreeable[9]?

I gotta say: I've been reading your sermons[10] and studying your books for six months now, and it feels like all I have to show for it is frustration and a sense of defeat. I swear I heard some girl ask "Why

---

1 elitist-ass: person that belongs to the elite group or class **2** threat: danger
3 black-on-black crime: crime in which the perpetrator and the victim are
people of color   **4** exploit (v): make unfair use of a person or situation
5 dish sth. out: present sth. in a thoughtless manner **6** mock (v): make fun of sb.
disrespectfully **7** remorseful: be sorry about sth. **8** offensive: making sb. feel
hurt or angry **9** agreeable: to sb.'s liking **10** sermon: part of a church service
where a speech on moral and religious topics is given

are black people so angry all the time?" as I left Blake's house, but how else am I supposed to feel?

My hand hurts. I'm going to bed.

—JM

CHAPTER 11

KNOCK KNOCK KNOCK.

Justyce rolls over onto his back and gropes[1] around for his cell phone. Squints[2] at the glaringly bright screen. Seventeen missed calls, four voice mails, and nine text messages from a combo of Manny, Mama, and Melo.   5

More knocking, then: "Jus? You in there?"

He groans[3]. "Justyce McAllister is unavailable, please leave a message."

"It's Dr. Dray, man. Open up."

Doc?   10

Justyce sits up too fast and his forehead smacks against something hard. *"Oww!"* he shouts.

"Jus, you all right?"

"Door's open," he says. Before his head clears[4] enough for him to figure out where he is and how he got here, Doc is squatting near his   15 feet. "Rough night?"

The underside of his mahogany desk swims[5] into focus.

So does the realization that his pants are around his shins[6].

"Oh shit!" He scrambles from beneath the desk and stands to pull them up, but his head throbs so intensely, he stumbles.   20

"Whoa there." Doc positions the desk chair behind him. "Have a seat."

Once he does, Doc pulls a bottle of Gatorade[7] from his bag and passes it to Jus. "Drink," he says. "All of it. I'm sure you're dehydrated."

Jus turns the bottle up. "What time is it?" he asks between swigs.   25

---

1 grope (v): search for sth. with your hands, not your eyes **2** squint (at sth.) (v): look at sth. through eyes that are partly closed **3** groan (v): making an indistinct sound that expresses pain **4** clear (v): (here) become less foggy **5** swim into focus: become visible **6** shin: *Schienbein* **7** Gatorade: sports drink

"According to that clock beside you, it's eleven-eleven." Doc smiles. "Make a wish. Or do kids not do that these days? I can't keep up with y'all."

Justyce peers[1] around the room. There's sunlight streaming through the pieces of tissue paper Braselton Preparatory Academy calls curtains. The thought of it makes his head throb again.

He also needs to throw up. "Uhh . . . 'Scuse[2] me," he says, falling out of the chair in the direction of the bathroom.

There goes the Gatorade.

He flushes, splashes some cold water on his face, and takes a good look in the mirror.

That's when it hits him: *Doc just found me under the desk in my dorm room with my pants down.*

Is he dreaming?

"Uhh . . . Doc? You still there?"

"Yep."

Jus gulps. "You, umm . . . got any plans for this fine Saturday?"

"Come on out here, Jus."

Dang it. "Do I have to?"

"No. But it'd definitely be in your best interests."

Jus takes himself in one more time and shakes his head. Doc is sitting with his elbows on his knees and his hands clasped[3] at the edge of Jus's perfectly made bed (which reminds Jus he didn't sleep in it. He shakes his head again). Doc smiles. Nods toward the desk chair. "Talk to me, Jus," he says once Justyce is seated.

Jus runs his hands down his face. "What do you want me to say?"

"Just wanna know what's up. I got a call from Manny a couple of hours ago. He's really worried about you."

Jus snorts.

Doc smiles. "He told me you'd do that."

"Whatever. That dude don't know me."

Doc's expression turns serious. "Tell me what happened, man."

---

1 peer (v): look concentrated and with difficulty at sb./sth. **2** 'scuse (infml): excuse **3** clasp (v): hold sth. tightly

"You mean Manny didn't tell you when he called to tattle[1] on me?"

Doc doesn't say a word to that. Just stares at Justyce with his piercing[2] green eyes. There's no judgment in them at all.

With Doc eyeing[3] him like that, last night floods Jus's memory, and the ache in his bruised knuckles[4] seems to intensify[5]. He drops his chin. "I messed up[6], Doc."

"How so?"

Jus looks up. "Manny really didn't tell you anything?"

Doc pulls his phone from his pocket, taps the screen a few times, then holds it up. Manny's voice pours[7] out of the speaker: *Mornin', Dr. Dray. Don't mean to bother you on a Saturday . . . I was wondering if you'd mind going by the dorm to check on Justyce. He's going through some things and I'm, uhh . . . Well, he's not answering his phone, and I'm sure he doesn't want to see me. If you could just pop[8] by there and make sure he's all right, I'd really appreciate it. Room two seventeen.*

"When I called him back to get more info," Doc says, "all he said was the two of you had a little to drink and there was a disagreement. He thought you could probably use someone to talk to."

Jus doesn't reply.

"So what's up, man? Why would Manny think you don't wanna see him?"

Justyce scratches his head. He needs a haircut. "I got drunk, Doc."

"I figured as much." Doc points to the empty Gatorade bottle.

"I got drunk and made the mistake of going to Blake Benson's house. Some stuff set[9] me off, and I just . . . I really messed up, man."

"Care[10] to expound?"

---

1 tattle (v): tell an authority about sb.'s bad actions **2** piercing (adj): penetrating
3 eye (v): watch sb. carefully **4** knuckle: *Fingerknöchel* **5** intensify: grow
stronger **6** mess up: ruin sth. by mistake **7** pour out: flow out of sth. freely
8 pop by (v): visit a place shortly and without notice **9** set sb. off: upset sb.
10 care to do sth: wish to do sth.

Justyce sighs. "Ever since my run-in[1] with that cop, I've been on high alert[2]. Noticing stuff I would've glossed[3] over or tried to ignore before."

"Makes sense."

5 "This might sound dumb, but I started this . . . project," Jus says. "For the past six months, I've been studying Dr. King's[4] stuff again and trying to apply[5] it? I've, uhh . . ." He looks up at Doc. Still no judgment there. "I've been writing letters to him in a notebook."

"That what's on your desk?"

10 Jus looks over his shoulder at the blue composition book with *Dear Martin* in the white space. "Yeah."

Doc nods. "Go on."

"Well, it was going fine, I guess, but then . . . Remember how I told you my dad passed when I was eleven?"

15 "Yes, I do."

"Well, he had PTSD[6] from the military and was an alcoholic. When he was alive, he would drink too much and go into these rages[7], and he, umm . . . well, he would hit my mom."

"I'm sorry to hear that, Jus."

20 Jus shrugs. "Was what it was. I caught a glimpse[8] of his eyes one time—there was nothing in them. It was almost like he wasn't even in his body, like his fists and feet were on autopilot and his brain had checked out."

Doc nods.

25 "I think something like that happened last night. I remember being pissed about some stuff in Blake's basement, and then he came over to me and Manny and said something that just pushed me over the edge. Words were exchanged, and then the next thing I remember, my hand was killing me, and Blake and Jared were get-

30 ting up from the floor."

---

1 run-in (infml): argument or conflict with sb. **2** be on high alert: constantly checking for possible danger **3** gloss over sth: downplay a serious problem as sth. unimportant **4** Dr. King: Martin Luther King Jr. (1929–1968) leader of the civil rights movement **5** apply sth.: use sth. **6** PTSD: post-traumatic stress disorder **7** rage: anger that is out of control **8** glimpse (n): short look at sth.

"I see."

"Yeah." Jus chuckles. "I feel like I shouldn't be tellin' you this because it's gonna get me expelled[1]."

"Sounds to me like you're 'taking responsibility.' That's tenet[2] four of the B-Prep honor code[3], isn't it?" Doc grins.

"I guess it is. Anyway, it's scary to think about now. The *last* person I ever wanna be like is my dad. Dude died in a fiery car crash with a blood-alcohol level of point two five. But last night I was *just* like him. I swear I'm never drinking again, man."

Doc laughs. "That's a good start."

"And then Manny . . ." Jus shakes his head. "I just don't get why he puts up with those *ass*holes—" He looks up. "Oh. Sorry."

Doc smiles. "It's okay. We're in your domain[4]. You were saying?"

"I know it's dumb, but when I hear him agree with those guys on stuff he *has* to know is wrong . . . I dunno, Doc."

Doc doesn't respond.

"Pretty sure I called him a sellout[5]," Jus says. "Right now, I'm still so mad at him, I don't even feel bad about it. I know he probably wasn't trying to take their side last night, but for him to get on *me* after the stuff Blake and Jared said? It's like he doesn't even care that they're disrespecting him. *Or* me."

Doc nods. "Mind if I play devil's advocate[6] for a sec? Don't want to dismiss your sentiments[7], just wanna give you a little perspective."

"Okay."

"So I grew up like Manny. Until I hit the tenth grade and transferred to a magnet academy[8] in the city, I was the only person of

---

1 expel: put a student out of a school forever 2 tenet: principle, belief
3 honor code: rulebook that is meant to shape the character development of students 4 domain: land, territory 5 sellout (infml): sb. who goes against their former group, does sth. they had promised not to do 6 devil's advocate: practice of offering an opposing opinion on an issue to provide a different perspective
7 sentiment: point of view 8 magnet academy: A magnet school is defined as an elementary, middle, or high school that offers a special curriculum capable of attracting large numbers of students of different social, economic, ethnic, and racial backgrounds.

color at my school. You remember how it felt to realize you only have so much control over how people see you?"

"How could I forget?" Jus rubs his wrists.

"That's what it was like for me at the new school. Everybody saw
5 me as black, even with the light skin and green eyes. The black kids expected me to know all the cultural references[1] and slang, and the white kids expected me to 'act' black. It was a rude[2] awakening[3] for me. When you spend your whole life being 'accepted' by white people, it's easy to ignore history and hard to face stuff that's still prob-
10 lematic, you feel me?"

"I guess."

"And as for you, the only way you're gonna thrive[4] is if you're okay with *yourself,* man. People are gonna disrespect you, but so what? Guys like Jared don't have any bearing on how far you get in life. If
15 *you* know the stuff they're saying isn't true, why let it bother you?"

Jus shakes his head. "I respect what you're saying, but it's not that simple."

"Go on."

"It's *frustrating,* man! When you work hard and earn your way,
20 and people suggest you haven't and you're not worthy, that shit hurts, Doc."

"Course it does, Jus. But who are you doing it for? Them? Or you?"

Jus puts his head in his hands.

"Another quick story," Doc says. "In grad school, I had this mas-
25 sive 'fro[5]. Usually wore it in cornrows. I'll never forget the way my doctoral advisor[6] frowned[7] when I stepped into his office for the first time. Throughout my entire PhD candidacy[8], he was hypercrit-

---

1 cultural reference: information that needs a specific cultural background to be understood **2** rude: offensive **3** awakening (n): becoming aware of sth.
4 thrive: live happily and multiply **5** 'fro: short for Afro, a style for curly hair, especially the natural curly hair many Black people have **6** doctoral advisor: person who helps PhD student with their scientific work **7** frown: facial expression that shows the person's dislike **8** PhD candidacy [ˌpiː eɪtʃ ˈdiː ˈkændɪdəsi]: time when university students write their doctoral thesis

ical[1] of my work. Told me to my face I'd never succeed. Jus, if I'd listened to him, I wouldn't be sitting here talking to you."

Justyce sighs.

"I'll let you get some rest," Doc says, rising from the bed. He puts another bottle of Gatorade and a ziplock bag with two pills in it on   5
the bedside table. "Got you some ibuprofen from the infirmary. Try to stay hydrated, all right?"

Justyce nods. "Thanks for coming by to check on me, Doc."

"Anytime, my man." Doc shakes Jus's shoulder.

As Doc pulls his bag strap across his chest and turns to leave,   10
Justyce glances over at his phone. Remembers all the missed calls and messages—and the lack thereof from a certain former debate partner.

"Doc, let me ask you something."

Doc turns and sticks his hands in his pockets. "Shoot[2]." "Do you . . . uhh . . ." *Am I really about to ask this?* "Do you have a girl-   15
friend?"

"Why do you ask?"

"Well . . ." What exactly is he supposed to say? "This about SJ?" Doc says.

Justyce's eyebrows lift.   20

Doc laughs. "You think I didn't notice the change between you two?"

"It sucks, Doc." Jus drops his chin.

"She'll come around[3]. Get some rest, okay?"

"Yeah. All right."   25

Jus gets up and goes over to fall on the bed as Doc pulls the door open.

He's asleep before he hears it click shut.

---

1 hypercritical [ˈhaɪpərkrɪtɪkl]: overly critical **2** shoot (v) (infml) (AE): (here) used to give permission to sb. to do or say sth. **3** come around: sb. changes or will change their mood/opinion

CHAPTER 12

On Tuesday, Manny and Jared are both missing from Societal Evolution.

Lunch too. Justyce sees Tyler, Kyle, and Blake—who scowls at Jus but keeps his distance—huddled[1] around a table in the senior
5 lounge, whispering.

As the day goes on, there's an ever-increasing buzz[2], though Justyce never catches what people are murmuring because they go quiet whenever he gets too close. So when he's walking to the dorm after classes are over and he sees the bros huddled around Jared's
10 car without Manny, he knows something is up.

Especially when Jared turns to give Jus the evil eye[3], and Jus sees his face.

Now, Jus knows he and Jared came to blows[4], but could he have caused *that* much damage? Dude looks like half his mug[5] got
15 attacked by a swarm of angry hornets.

When he gets back to his room, Justyce does the unthinkable: he calls Manny.

Of course the guy doesn't answer.

There's a knock at the door. "Come in," Jus says, dropping down
20 into his desk chair. As he pulls out his notebook to skim the letter he wrote Martin after Blake's party, he hears the door open and close before the bedsprings[6] squeak[7].

When he turns around, he almost falls out of the chair. "Dawg!"

---

1 huddle (v): stay close together **2** buzz: humming, murmuring **3** the evil eye: superstitious idea that you can harm or hurt other people by looking at them in a special way **4** come to blows: pick a fight and hit each other **5** mug (n): face **6** bedspring: spring that gives support to the mattress **7** squeak (v): make a shrill sound

Manny is stretched out on Justyce's bed with his hands tucked behind his head. His left hand is all taped[1] up, and it appears one of Jared's hornets got him in the upper lip.

"Whoa," Jus says.

Manny just stares at the ceiling.   5

Something pops into Jus's head: Manny pushing open the passenger door of the Range Rover and telling him to get in.

"Hey, man, I—"

"Save it. I know you didn't mean it."

Mmmm . . . "Actually, I did," Jus says.   10

Manny shifts his attention to Jus and lifts his eyebrows.

"I just didn't really consider the bigger picture," Jus says. "*That's* what I'm apologizing for. Not putting myself in your shoes[2] or whatever."

Manny turns back to the ceiling. "I didn't really have your best   15
interests in mind either, so let's call it even[3] and move on."

Jus nods. "Cool."

After about half a minute, the silence gets awkward. Jus cracks his knuckles. "So what happened to your lip?"

"I woke up."   20

"Okay . . ." Jus decides to take a page from Doc's book: "Care to expound a bit?"

Manny smiles but then grimaces in pain. After a few seconds, he sits up and turns to face Justyce. "You know why I couldn't really get mad about what you said? You were right. I *knew* you were right the   25
moment the words came outta your mouth."

"Oh," Jus says.

"Saturday night, I went to a festival with those clowns. Four times, man—*four*—I had to grit my teeth to keep from knocking Jared's punk ass out. Every time he made fun of somebody, it was   30
like sandpaper being dragged over my eardrums."

---

1 tape up: covered with bandages **2** put yourself in sb.'s shoes: think about sb.'s situation from their perspective **3** call it even (infml): when two people agree they both did sth. wrong to the other

"Dang."

"When we saw this black lady with four kids, and this fool called her Shaniqua[1] and made a joke about baby daddies, I couldn't take any more, Jus. I called him on it, and he rolled his eyes. Told me to
5   'stop being so fucking sensitive.' "

Jus doesn't say anything.

"All day Sunday, I sat in my basement, just fuming[2]. I think I listened to Deuce Diggs and played *Medal of Honor*[3] for like six hours straight. The whole time, all I could think about was how I said the
10   same thing to *you*. How right you were. How good of a friend you've been—"

"All right with all that soft stuff, Manny."

"I'm serious, Jus. Them fools don't wanna hear when they're being offensive. They couldn't care less[4] what it's like to live in our
15   skin. Those assholes aren't my damn *friends*."

Jus doesn't know what to say.

Wait, yes he does. "So, umm . . ." He gestures to Manny's wrapped hand and busted lip. "Those?"

Manny smiles. "This morning I went in to tell Coach I quit—"
20   *"Huh?"*

"Dawg, I *hate* playin' basketball. Only reason I started is cuz when you're the tall black kid at school, that's what people expect you to do. Yeah, I happen to be pretty good at it, but it's really not my thing."

"Okay, then."
25   "Anyway, Jared was in Coach's office. When I said I was quitting, he made a 'joke' about how I couldn't until *Massah*[5] set me free. I lost it." Manny falls back on the bed. "He clipped[6] me once, but I can't even tell you how good it felt to pound[7] that dude. Coach

---

1 Shaniqua (sl) (derog): a name used as an offensive, racist stereotype to say that a Black woman is loud, uneducated, has sex with too many partners, etc.
2 fume (v) [fju:m]: show anger and frustration **3** *Medal of Honor*: a computer game based on fighting in war **4** you could not care less: you are totally indifferent **5** massah: historically used by slaves to address their master and owner
6 clip sb. (v): hit sb. **7** pound sb. (v): punch sb. repeatedly

wanted to keep it on the low[1] cuz he needs Jared to play in tomorrow's game, so he sent me home and made Jared stay in his office till school let out[2]."

"Well, damn."

Manny sits back up. "I just wanna thank you, man."   5

"For what?"

"For helping me get my eyes open. Didn't like what I saw, so I wanted to shut 'em again, but if it wasn't for you, I wouldn't know some of the stuff I've always felt around those guys is legit[3]."

"Okay ... You're welcome, I guess?"   10

Manny stands and opens his arms. "Bring[4] it in, fella."

"What?"

"Man, getcho[5] ass up and give ya boy a hug."

"You really creep me out sometimes, Manny," Jus says, complying[6].

---

1 keep it on the low (sl) (AE): not let people know about sth. **2** let out: finish
3 legit (adj): true **4** bring it in (sl): a way of telling sb. to hug you **5** getcho (sl):
get your **6** comply: act accordingly

January 23

I've got a lot on my mind, Martin.

Last night, Manny's dad came down to the basement. In almost four years of hanging out at the Rivers' house, I've never seen Mr. Julian
5 in Manny's "sacred[1] space," as he calls it, so when he dropped down between us on the sofa, it felt like a bomb was about to go off.

For a good three minutes, it was dead silent[2]. Then Mr. Julian sighed. "I wanna talk to you boys," he said.

I gulped, and glanced at Manny behind Mr. Julian's head. He looked
10 hella[3] nervous too. "Uhh . . . sure, Dad."

Mr. Julian nodded. "Today I overheard[4] an employee refer to me by a racial slur[5]."

"For real?" I said.

"Yep. White kid, few years post-undergrad. I hired[6] him
15 three months ago."

Manny looked pissed[7]. "What'd he call you?"

"Doesn't matter, son. Point is, it reminded me of your recent[8] run-in with Jared. I spent the rest of the day wondering if you being in that situation was my fault."

20 "Huh? How the heck could it be your fault, Dad?"

(I was wondering the same thing, Martin.)

"There's a lot I haven't told you, Emmanuel," Mr. Julian said. "Not sure if I was trying to shield[9] you or if I hoped things were better, but it's something I've been thinking about since Justyce was unfairly arrested."
25 He turned to me. "The whole incident came as a shock, right?"

"Yeah. It did."

"When that happened, I kept thinking: What if that had been you, Emmanuel? I know you would've been downright[10] mind-blown[11] . . .

---

1 sacred: holy **2** dead silent: completely silent **3** hella (infml) [AE]: extremely, very **4** overhear: hear sth./sb. by accident or chance **5** slur (n): insult **6** hire sb. (v): employ a person **7** pissed (sl): frustrated, angry **8** recent (adj): just a short while ago **9** shield sb. (v): offer protection to sb. **10** downright (adv): completely **11** mind-blowing (adj): overwhelming on an emotional or psychological level

but I wouldn't've[1]." He shook his head. "That didn't sit[2] right with me because as your father, it's something I should've prepared you for, son. And Jared saying what he said? I should've prepared you for that too."

"No offense[3], Mr. Julian," I said, "but my mama's been 'preparing' me for as long as I can remember. I was still caught off guard[4]."   5

"You were surprised by what Jared said to Manny?"

"Oh. Uhh . . . not really," I said.

"Exactly. That's what I'm talking about. I wasn't surprised to hear that kid at the office today say what he said. There's no predicting people's actions, but you can be prepared to face certain attitudes. Perhaps 10 if I'd been more open with my own experiences, Jared's words wouldn't have been so astonishing[5] to Manny."

Neither of us responded.

"Both of you know what I do for a living," he went on, "but very few know my struggle to get there. It took me four years longer than 15 average to secure my position because I was continuously overlooked[6] for promotions. I worked much harder than many of my Caucasian[7] colleagues but rarely received a fraction[8] of the recognition[9]."

Again, we kept quiet.

"There are still people in that office who refuse to look me in the eye, 20 fellas. They'll show cursory[10] respect for the sake of keeping their jobs, but a good majority of my subordinates[11] resent[12] having to answer to a black man. I was reminded of that today."

"You fired that guy, right?" Manny asked.

---

1 wouldn't've (infml): would not have **2** sit right with sth./sb.: feel right/suitable in sb.'s opinion **3** no offense (infml): used to show that sth. negative may be said but the speaker does not want to cause insult or hurt **4** off guard: being not prepared for sth. **5** astonishing: amazing, shocking **6** overlook sb./sth. (v): not taking notice of sb./sth. **7** Caucasian [kɔːˈkeɪʒn] (adj) (AE): belonging to one of the groups of people who have pale skin, 'white' US Americans **8** fraction of sth.: small amount of sth. **9** recognition: paying respect to sb.'s skills, achievements or knowledge **10** cursory [ˈkɜːrsəri]: superficial, done quickly without attention to detail **11** subordinate (n): person who has a position with less authority and power than sb. else in an organization **12** resent sth./sb. [rɪˈzent]: feel angry or bitter about sth., esp. because you think it is unfair

Mr. Julian shook his head. "It's not the first time it's happened, and it won't be the last. This is what I mean by preparation."

Manny was livid. "But, Dad—"

"The young man knows I heard what he said. I have no doubt he'll
5 be on his best behavior going forward. People often learn more from getting an undeserved pass[1] than they would from being punished."

"That's kinda deep," I said.

He shrugged. "Kill 'em with kindness. My point is the world is full of guys like Jared and that employee, and most of them will never change.
10 So it's up to you fellas to push through it. Probably best not to talk with your fists in the future . . ." He nudged Manny. "But at least you have an idea of what you're up against. Try not to let it stop you from doing your best, all right?"

He rubbed both of our heads and got up to leave.

15 I haven't been able to stop thinking about it, Martin. Frankly, it's pretty discouraging. To think Mr. Julian has all that authority and still gets disrespected? Hearing it made me realize I still had hope that once I really achieve some things, I won't have to deal with racist BS[2] anymore.

20 That's obviously not the case, though, is it? What do I do with that? I have no doubt you would've done exactly what Mr. Julian did, but if it had been me? Well . . .

I mean I punched a guy for using the n-word recently, didn't I?

The conversation reminded me of something Doc asked me a few
25 days ago: all the work I'm doing to try and get ahead in life, who am I doing it for?

Better yet, what am I doing it for? To prove myself? Gain some respect? Be able to shove it in the faces of people like Jared?

I don't even know anymore, Martin.

30 (Side note: Don't ask about SJ. Still getting cold-shouldered. It's whatever.)

—J

1 undeserved pass: when sb. is surprisingly not punished for their bad behaviour
2 BS (sl): bullshit

CHAPTER 13

Jus knows something's wrong the moment he climbs into Manny's car Saturday morning. Which is kind of unfortunate because it's a really nice day. The guys are supposed to be hitting[1] Stone Mountain, but if Manny's holey wife-beater[2], flannel[3] pajama[4] pants, house slippers, and scowl are any indication, hiking isn't real high on his to-do list at the moment.

"You mind if we just drive for a while?" Manny asks once Justyce's door is closed.

"Course not, man. What's goin' on?"

Jus gets his seat belt fastened, and Manny pulls out of the lot[5]. "My folks got a call this morning. Mr. Christensen is pressing charges[6] against me for 'assaulting[7]' his son." He takes his hand off the wheel to do the air quotes[8].

"You serious, man?"

"As a heart attack. I tried to get in touch with Jared, but Mr. Christensen answered his phone and told me not to call anymore. Said they'd take out a restraining order[9] if I did."

Justyce is dumbfounded[10]. "Dawg, that is some straight bullshit."

"You tellin' me, man. I've never seen my dad so fired up." Manny shakes his head. "All those years that man has looked me in my face and called me his 'other son,' and this is what happens."

"I don't even know what to say, man."

---

1 hit sth. (v) (infml): travel to a place **2** wife-beater (infml): undershirt without sleeves **3** flannel (adj): soft wool fabric **4** pajamas: sleeping outfit **5** lot: parking lot, place where cars are parked **6** press charges: take sb. to court for a crime **7** assault sb. (v): physically attack sb. **8** air quotes (infml): gesturing quotation marks to indicate irony or mockery of what is about to be said **9** restraining order: court ordering sb. to stop contacting or approaching sb. **10** dumbfounded (adj): astonished, amazed

"You know what? I really don't either. I've had my little awakening over the past week or whatever, but *this* is like . . . Man, I wasn't prepared for this. All I can think about is that one Socio Evo chat where SJ said Jared and me could do the same crime, but *I'm* likely to get the harsher punishment. You remember that?"

"I do." How could he forget?

"Anyway, sorry about Stone Mountain. I just need to drive and clear my head a bit."

"All good, Manny. All good."

Jus settles down into the seat and enjoys the wind in his face as Manny turns on some music.

> **So catch that ball, Nigga; shoot that shot.**
> **Put on them gloves, Boy; knock off ya brotha's block.**
> **Lace up them track spikes[1]; get ready to run.**
> **Here comes the fun, wait for the sound of the gun . . .**

"This the new Deuce Diggs?" Jus asks.

"Yeah, dawg. Shit's poppin'[2]."

"Crank[3] that up."

Manny turns it up so loud, the whole car shakes from the bass.

When the Range Rover rolls to a stop at a traffic light, Jus looks out his window to find the driver of a white Suburban—white dude, probably early fifties—giving him a dirty look.

He turns the music down. "Damn . . . dude over here is muggin[4] *hard*."

Manny checks the guy out and laughs. "Homeboy's[5] got no appreciation for a lyrical genius such as Deuce Diggs."

"Apparently not," Justyce says, shifting in his seat. The way the guy's scowling at him reminds him a *little* too much of The Incident. "Man, these red lights are long as hell."

---

1 lace up them track spikes (sl): put on your running shoes **2** shit's poppin' (sl): sth. is hitting hard **3** crank sth. up: increase the volume **4** mugging (sl): stare at sb. intensely **5** homeboy (sl): very close friend

"You right, dawg."

When it finally turns green, Manny turns the music back up.

The white Suburban is riding alongside the guys now, and the driver seems pissed. "This dude is giving me the creeps[1]!" Jus yells over the music. "He's red as a pepper, and he keeps glaring at me with those bulgy eyeballs[2]."

"I bet he's totally profiling us right now. Probably thinks we're drug dealers or something."

Justyce's eyes go to his wrists, and Manny glances over and stops laughing. "My bad, dawg," he says. "I didn't mean . . . Sorry, I wasn't thinkin'."

"It's all good, Manny. You're prolly right."

They pull to a stop at the Thirteenth Street traffic light.

"Will you assholes turn that goddamn racket[3] down!" the guy in the Suburban shouts.

"Assholes?" Jus says. "How are we assholes?"

Manny leans over the center console[4] to shout out Jus's window: "What'd you say, sir? I couldn't hear you over the music!"

The guy looks like he's about to ignite[5]. "I SAID TURN THAT SHIT DOWN!"

"You weren't lying about him being red!" Manny laughs. "It's like all the blood in his body has rushed up into his face."

Jus turns to the man again.

What would Martin do, Jus?

"Maybe we should turn it down," Jus says.

"Man, please. This is *my* car," Manny says. "I'm done bending over backwards[6] to appease[7] white people." He pushes a button on the steering wheel, and the music gets louder.

"YOU WORTHLESS NIGGER SONS OF BITCHES!" the guy shouts.

---

1 give sb. the creeps: making sb. fearful, uncomfortable or nervous **2** bulgy eyeballs (infml): *Glotzaugen* **3** racket (n): loud, unpleasant noise **4** center console: divider between the driver's seat and the passenger's seat **5** ignite: set on fire **6** bend over backwards: try extremely hard **7** appease: being kind to an aggressive person in order to keep the peace

"I *know* that muthafucka didn't just say what I think he did," Manny says.

Jus's heart jumps up between his ears.

What would Martin do what would Martin do what would
5 *Martin—?*

"Forget that guy, Manny. Let's just stay calm—"

"Naw, man. Screw that." Manny leans over Jus. "Hey, fuck you, man!" he shouts out the window, giving the guy the finger.

"Manny, chill." *Why is this damn light so long?* "Let's just turn it
10 down till we get away from this guy, all right?"

Justyce leans forward to reach for the volume knob[1]. "Oh *SHIT*!" Manny shouts—

---

1 volume knob: device to turn the loudness down or up

CHAPTER 14

BANG.

BANG.

BANG.

PART TWO

Transcript[1] from evening news, January 26

Good evening, and welcome to the Channel 5 News at 5.

In our top story, tragedy in Oak Ridge this afternoon, where two young men in an SUV were shot at a traffic light. The incident occurred[2] just after noon at the inter-section[3] of Thirteenth Street and Marshall Avenue. According to the wife of the shooter—who was riding in the passenger seat—there was a brief dispute[4] over loud music before shots were fired from one vehicle into the other.

The identities of the wounded[5] are being withheld[6] pending[7] further investigation, but we've received reports that one of the teens was pronounced[8] dead en route[9] to the hospital, and the other is in critical condition[10].

The shooter has been identified as fifty-two-year-old Garrett Tison, an officer with the Atlanta PD. Officer Tison was not on duty at the time of the shooting and was taken into police custody[11] at the scene.

More on this story as it continues to develop.

---

1 transcript: written copy **2** occur: happen **3** intersection: place where two roads meet **4** dispute (n): argument **5** wounded ['wuːndɪd]: injured **6** withhold sth.: not share sth., usu. information **7** pending: happening after sth. else happens first **8** be pronounced dead: be officially declared dead **9** en route: on the way **10** critical condition: live-threatening condition **11** police custody: prison

February 1

DEAR MARTIN,

He's gone.
   Never did anything to anyone, and now Manny's gone.

5   I can't do this anymore.

CHAPTER 15

Twenty-seven days.

That's how long the Riverses keep Manny's body in a mortuary[1] cold chamber, waiting for his best friend to recover enough to attend the funeral[2]. Frankly, Jus wishes they'd gone ahead and had it without him. He really doesn't wanna be here.

The first words out of the pastor's[3] mouth were "We are not here to mourn[4] a death. We're here to celebrate a life, gone on to glory." Manny didn't even believe in heaven and hell. Jus can imagine him saying: *The only place I've "gone on" to is that overpriced[5] casket[6].*

Jus didn't have it in him to go up and look at the body during the viewing. He knows the cause of death—"gunshot wound to the head"—because he asked to see the death certificate, and the Riverses consented[7]. To see Manny laid out[8] all serene[9] after knowing there was a bullet somewhere in his head? Yeah, there's no way. Jus can't do that.

He would love to just get up and walk out. Keep going until his legs fall off or he dies from thirst or starvation[10] or exhaustion or some combination of the three. Problem is there are media people everywhere outside. Based on some of the "speculation[11]" he's heard—Manny threatened Garrett Tison, one of the boys threw something into Tison's Suburban, Justyce had a gun, etc.—he'd rather not be seen.

---

1 mortuary ['mɔːtʃəri]: place where dead bodies are stored until they are buried or burned **2** funeral: ceremony that is held when sb. has died **3** pastor: head of a Christian church **4** mourn [mɔːn]: show your grief when sb. has died **5** overpriced: when sth. has a higher price than what it is worth **6** casket: coffin; a box in which a dead body is buried or cremated **7** consent (v): permit sth. to happen **8** lay out: put on display **9** serene: peaceful **10** starvation: hunger **11** speculation: forming opinions about events and their causes without having the facts

Not that being inside is much better. People keep peeping[1] over
their shoulders at him where he's sitting at the back of the church
with Mama. He has sunglasses on, but he can see them sneaking
glances[2]. Marveling[3] at the Boy Who Survived (that's what they've
5 been calling him on the news).

Mama squeezes his good arm. He's still relearning how to use his
other one, which is currently in a sling. The shot to the chest cracked
a rib and punctured[4] his right lung, but the bullet he took to the
right shoulder messed up a bunch of nerves. After three surgeries[5],
10 he finally regained[6] feeling in his fingertips.

As the pastor leaves the pulpit[7] and the choir stands, Justyce
looks around the packed interior of the church. He takes in[8] all the
dark suits and dresses, the tearstained[9] faces and shaking shoulders,
and the collective sorrow[10] hits him so hard, the room blurs out
15 of focus. The one thing he *can* see clearly is the face of Sarah-Jane
Friedman. She's watching him.

It triggers a series of flashbacks[11] from his more heavily drugged[12]
days in the hospital: SJ standing over him, weeping[13], his left hand
gripped[14] in her right one, her left hand stroking[15] his face (Mama
20 was obviously *not* around); the sound of Dr. Rivers saying, "We're
so glad you made it, Justyce." Mama crying and asking his forgiveness[16] because she had to go back to work. Melo being escorted[17]
out because she wouldn't stop wailing[18].

---

1 peep (n): taking a quick look **2** sneaking glances: getting a secret look at sth./
sb. **3** marvel at sth. (v): be surprised and filled with wonder about sth.
4 puncture (v): pierce **5** surgery ['sɜːdʒəri]: medical operation **6** regain: get sth.
back that you have lost **7** pulpit: place in a church from where a pastor preaches
8 take sth. in: understand/accept sth./a situation by looking at it fully
9 tearstained: having visible marks of tears from crying **10** sorrow (n): feeling
of loss **11** flashback (n): unexpected and sudden memory of a past event
12 drugged: being under the influence of drugs **13** weep (v): cry **14** grip (v):
take hold of sth. **15** stroke (v): gently move your hand over sb.'s hair or skin
16 forgiveness: the act of not holding sb. responsible/being no longer angry at
sb. for doing sth. bad to you **17** escort (v): accompany sb. safely to a place
18 wail (v): cry loudly

Speaking of Melo, Jus can see her too. Honestly, if it weren't for Mama, he's sure she'd try to glue[1] herself to his side. *She* organized the group of Atlanta Falcons football players who came to escort Jus home from the hospital in a luxury party bus.

Of course it made the news.   5

As Mr. Rivers approaches the pulpit to deliver the eulogy[2]—he asked Jus if he wanted to do it, but there was no way in hell—Jus sees Jared and the "bros." They're all sitting near the front with their parents, and he wonders if Jared and Mr. Christensen feel like the assholes they are. If it hadn't been for that damn phone call, Manny   10 and Jus would've been headed to Stone Mountain. They wouldn't have been on the same road as Garrett Tison.

Manny would still be here.

Jared turns around like he can feel Jus jabbing[3] arrows into the back of his head. The moment they see each other (though Jared   15 wouldn't know because of Justyce's sunglasses), fury wraps[4] around Jus so tightly, he almost can't breathe. Even from a distance, Jus can tell Jared's eyes are haunted[5]. Like the floor has opened up beneath him and there's no bottom to his agony[6].

Jus recognizes the expression because he's feeling the same way.   20 It makes him want to burn the world down.

* * *

Once the service is over, Jus walks with Mama to the bathroom before they head to the burial site[7] (he doesn't want to go). As soon as she steps in, who steps out but Sarah-Jane Friedman. His mouth falls open a little, and when she sees him, she freezes.   25

Jus takes his sunglasses off. She's in a navy pantsuit, no makeup, dark hair pulled back into a bun. Her eyes—which are red from cry-

---

1 glue yourself to sb./sth.: stay very close to sb./sth. **2** eulogy [ˈjuːlədʒi]: speech given at a funeral to praise the dead person **3** jab (v): stab **4** wrap (v): cover
5 haunted: very worried and troubled **6** agony: great pain **7** burial site: place where the dead are being buried

ing—rove[1] over his face, and he's so relieved[2] to see something other than pity[3] burning in them, he almost reaches out to hug her with his good arm.

It's quite the predicament[4]: wanting to touch and hug and kiss
5 a white girl after a white man shot him and killed his best friend?

"Hey," he says.

Her eyes fill with tears. "Hey."

"You okay?"

"Pretty sure that's what I should be asking *you*, Jus."

10 He looks away. Shrugs.

Moments pass that feel like hours. Days. Years. Centuries.

She sighs. "So I know we haven't talked much bu—"

"I miss you, S."

Her head snaps up[5].

15 "I mean it," Jus says. And why shouldn't he tell her? He's already lost his other best friend.

SJ opens her mouth to speak—

The ladies' room door opens. "You ready, Just—?" Mama sees SJ. "Oh, I'm sorry. Didn't realize you were speaking with someone."

20 "Ma, this is Sarah-Jane," Jus says, never taking his eyes off SJ.

Mama: Lovely to meet you.

SJ: Same to you, Ms. McAllister.

Mama turns to Justyce. "I'm gonna head on out to the car. You coming?"

25 "I'll meet you there," he says. "I want to walk SJ out."

"No, no. You don't have to. My parents are actually waiting for me. I'll see you at the grave site?"

"Oh. Yeah. Okay. Bye, S."

"Bye, Jus."

---

1 rove (v): wander around **2** relieved: being no longer in fear or distress
3 pity (n): feeling sorry for sb's suffering **4** predicament [prɪˈdɪkəmənt]: awkward
situation **5** snap up: moves quickly up

As SJ disappears around the corner, Mama's expression shifts to a frown. "Sarah-Jane, huh? You know her from school or something?"

"She's my debate partner, Ma. I've mentioned her plenty of times."

"Hmph. I saw how she was looking at you. More on that girl's mind than *debate*—"

"Can we not start with this at my best friend's funeral, please?"

"I'm not starting with anything, Justyce. Just sayin' watch yourself with that one. That's all."

That one.

"She's a good friend, Ma."

"And you'd do well to keep it that way."

Jus wants to argue. He wants to tell Mama all the ways SJ made him believe he was big while everyone else wanted to keep him small. He wants to call Mama on *her* prejudice. Tell her, in his mind, she's just as bad as the guy who shot him and Manny.

But he doesn't get a chance to.

The second he and Mama step out of the church, they get mobbed[1] by reporters.

Mr. McAllister, how's[2] it feel to be the Boy Who Survived?

Justyce, do you think there will be justice?

What's it like knowing it could've been YOU in that casket?

That last one sets Justyce off. "Do YOU have to be such an asshole, man?"

"Justyce, don't say another word," Mama says, then to the reporters: "My son has no comment. Now if you'll excuse us . . ."

She uses an arm to sweep a smaller reporter out of the way, then grabs Justyce by his elbow to pull him through the gap. Mr. Taylor shouts and points in their direction, and suddenly he and Mama get flanked by what have to be bodyguards.

---

1 get mobbed by sb./sth.: when people aggressively approach you from all sides
2 how's (infml): how does

Justyce winces[1] as one of the huge guys—burly[2], blond, looks like his name could be Lars—bumps[3] his bad arm. The pain that shoots from his shoulder through his entire body like a bolt of lightning is nothing compared to what's inside him.

---

1 wince (v): when your face muscle tightens because you feel pain **2** burly: broad-shouldered and strongly built **3** bump (v): knock or run into sth./sb.

Tison Indictment
Step Forward for Justice or
Grand Jury Blunder[1]?

By: Tobias D'bitru
Staff Writer

5

Yesterday afternoon, a Georgia grand jury returned a multiple-count[2] indictment against former Atlanta police officer Garrett Tison in connection with a January shooting involving two teenaged boys. The indictment stands in glaring[3] contrast to the Nevada and Florida cases involving the 10 deaths of Shemar Carson and Tavarrius Jenkins, and two of the charges—aggravated[4] assault and felony murder[5]—have many members of the community in an uproar[6].

"The man was defending himself from thugs," said Tison's neighbor April Henry. "I've known Garrett for twenty-five 15 years. If he says those boys had a gun, they had a gun." A fellow police officer, who asked to remain anonymous, claims the indictment is nothing more than a publicity stunt[7] at Tison's expense[8]. "They're out to make an example of him. Prosecutor[9] pulled the race card, and the grand jury 20 bought it hook, line, and sinker[10]."

And many agree. At a solidarity rally held in Tison's honor, picketers[11] wore T-shirts that read "Race-Baiting[12] Should Be

---

1 blunder: a stupid or careless mistake **2** multiple-count: containing more than one criminal charge **3** glaring (adj): very obvious to the point that it is suspicious **4** aggravated: serious **5** felony murder (fml): when the killing of a person is seen as a murder and serious crime **6** uproar: a situation where there is a lot of negative public feeling and anger at sth. **7** publicity stunt: sth. that is done in order to attract attention **8** expense (n): cost **9** prosecutor: public law officer who presses charges against sb. and represents the public in court **10** hook, line, sinker: phrase that emphasizes that sb. has been completely tricked but does not know it **11** picketer: protestor **12** race-baiting: calling members of a racial group names

a Crime" while holding signs featuring Tison's face and the words "Protector[1] not Poster Child[2]."

A trial date[3] has yet to be announced.

---

1 protector: sb. who protects and defends you against sth./sb. 2 poster child: sb. who is seen as a (positive) representative of a campaign, movement, etc.
3 trial date: day on which trial in court begins

CHAPTER 16

Two days after being permanently set free from his sling[1], Justyce gets to drive his brand-new car. Ken Murray, owner of seven Honda dealerships[2] across the city, is the father of one of Jus's classmates, and Jus found a Civic[3] with *Condolences*[4] *from the Murray Honda Family* on the windshield the day he came home from the hospital.

At first, he wanted to give it back—the idea of driving around in a free car from some rich white dude made him sick to his stomach considering what had happened. But after staring at it for weeks and rereading[5] the *Neither of you young men deserved what happened* letter from Mr. Murray, Jus decided to accept the gift.

It's been a month and a half since the shooting, but going to Manny's house now is no easier today than it would've been the day he learned Manny was gone. The Riverses invited Justyce to dinner tonight to "commemorate[6]" Garrett Tison's indictment, but Jus really isn't looking forward to being alone with them. Especially not inside their house. The more he thinks about it—and he's been thinking about it a lot lately—it wasn't the house that felt like a second home to him. It was Manny.

As he pulls into the driveway[7], Jus instinctively heads toward door three of the four-car garage. He can remember all the times he and Manny waited for it to rise before pulling inside, and his stomach crawls up into his throat.

Before he can throw his car in reverse[8] and get outta there, door three *does* rise, and Mr. Rivers motions for Justyce to pull in. The

---

1 sling (v): soft strap that supports a broken arm and is looped around the neck
2 car dealership: place where cars are sold **3** Honda Civic: Japanese car
4 condolence: words of sympathy spoken to family/friends of sb. who has died
5 reread: read again **6** commemorate sth.: show your respect for sb./sth. by
remembering **7** driveway: short way leading up to a garage **8** in reverse:
prepare to drive backwards by shifting gears

spot is empty, of course—Range Rover's long gone—but there's no way Jus can fill it. He puts his car in park in the driveway and climbs out. " 'Preciate[1] it, Mr. Julian, but I can't," he says.

Manny's dad smiles sadly and looks over the space. "It's just so empty, you know? Come on in."

When Jus steps inside and the fragrance[2] of chicken cacciatore assaults his senses, he's one hundred percent sure he doesn't wanna be here. He doesn't wanna sit down at the antique oak[3] table to eat from the "special-occasion" dishes Dr. Rivers has taken from her china[4] cabinet. He doesn't wanna make small talk with his dead best friend's parents as they eat *his* favorite meal and not their son's.

All of this is way too much, and he wants to leave and never come back.

He steps into the dining room anyway.

"Thank you for coming, sweetheart," Dr. Rivers says, pulling Jus into what has to be the most emotion-filled hug he's ever experienced. He counts a full seventeen seconds before she lets go.

"Thanks for having me," he replies.

"Go ahead and sit," Mr. Julian says. "I'll get you something to drink."

Jus does as instructed, and after a minute, Mr. Julian comes to the table with three beverages: a glass of red wine for Dr. Rivers, a glass of iced tea for Justyce, and a tumbler[5] of what Jus assumes is Jack Daniel's Single Barrel—that's the stuff Manny used to sneak into his flask—for himself.

Just seeing it makes Jus want to vomit[6].

"So how you holdin' up[7], Justyce?" Mr. Julian says once[8] seated. "Back in school yet?"

Jus shakes his head. "Not quite. I move into the dorm on Sunday and start classes Monday."

---

1 'preciate (infml): appreciate **2** fragrance: lovely smell **3** oak: Eiche
4 china: fine white ceramic dishes **5** tumbler: glass usu. used for drinking
whiskey **6** vomit (v): throw up **7** hold up: stay strong in a very difficult situation
8 once: as soon as sth./sb. is/was

"I see."

Dr. Rivers comes in holding an oval dish with two potholders[1]. She sets it on the table, and the chicken breasts and legs smothered[2] in mushrooms and red sauce stare up at Justyce. "You think you're ready?" she says.   5

"Ready as I'll ever be, I guess." Jus shrugs. "I'm caught up, but it's now or never if I want to graduate in May."

She nods and heads back to the kitchen. Returns with a dish full of jasmine rice with three chunks of butter melting into it. "Pass me your plate."   10

Jus complies.

"We're really happy you came to join us tonight," Mr. Julian says. "Means a lot to us."

Dr. Rivers hands Jus his plate, loaded up with food he has no appetite for. "We're not expecting you to talk much," she says. "Just   15
nice to have your presence is all."

"Thank you. Yours too." A lie, but it seems the right thing to say.

The three descend[3] into silence as silverware[4] clinks[5] and scrapes against bone china[6] and beverages slowly disappear from glasses. Justyce is thankful for the lack of conversation; Manny's absence   20
makes it almost impossible to breathe, let alone talk.

Once they finish, Mr. Julian clears his throat. "So, Justyce, we invited you here tonight for a few reasons," he begins.

Justyce picks up his glass and gulps down[7] the rest of his tea.

"The first, of course, is to memorialize[8] the indictment," Mr. Julian   25
goes on. "We won't dwell[9] on it, but to us—and surely to you as well—it *is* something to commemorate."

Dr. Rivers nods. "It's not a conviction, of course. But it's a start. Just a relief to know what happened is being treated as a crime."

---

1 potholder: fabric used to hold hot dishes **2** smother in/with: cover sth. with sth. completely **3** descend into silence: nobody talks **4** silverware: forks, knifes, spoons etc. that are made of silver **5** clink (v): sound made when striking metal or ceramic **6** bone china: special ceramic **7** gulp down: drink or eat sth. up very quickly **8** memorialize: keep the memory of sb./sth. alive **9** dwell on sth.: speak in detail and at length about sth. that is sad and frustrating

Jus stares at the gilt edge[1] around his plate. "Yeah," he says. "That is a relief."

"Moving on," Dr. Rivers says. "The second reason: I'm not sure if you remember Emmanuel's cousin—Quan Banks?"

5 Justyce's head jerks up.

"He says you went to elementary school together. Is that correct?"

"It is," Jus says. "But I had no idea he and Manny were cousins until . . ." He pauses. "Until Quan got arrested."

10 She nods. "Well, if you're willing, Quan would like to see you. You've been added to his visitation list[2]."

"Oh. Okay . . ."

"Emmanuel's death hit him pretty hard. You don't have to visit, of course"—she and Mr. Julian do that married thing where they
15 communicate with a glance—"but he says you're the only person he wants to talk to."

"I see." Though he really doesn't.

"If you're interested, I'll give you the information before you leave."

20 Jus doesn't know what to say. Quan wants to see *him*? "Okay. Sounds good." Another lie.

For a minute, no one speaks. Jus can feel Mr. Julian's gaze, but there's no way he can look at him. He's what Manny would've looked like if he'd gotten the chance to get older.

25 "There's one more thing." Dr. Rivers's voice wavers[3]. "Julian?"

"Yeah, okay."

Mr. Julian gets up from the table and walks over to the china cabinet. Opens it and pulls out a black box. He sets it on the table in front of Justyce. "We intended to give this to Emmanuel for his eigh-
30 teenth birthday," he says. "I have no doubt[4] he'd want you to have it

---

1 gilt edge: sth. that has a thin layer of gold covering its edges **2** visitation list: list of people that are allowed to visit a person in jail **3** waver: shake slightly
4 no doubt: used to express that the speaker is absolutely sure

under these circumstances, so we'd be honored if you'd receive it in his stead[1]."

Jus stares at the box, afraid to move, let alone touch it.

Dr. Rivers clears her throat, and he lifts his head. She smiles, though there are tears in her eyes. "Go on." 5

Jus takes the box off the table and lifts the hinged top. By some miracle, he manages not to drop the contents on the floor and run away screaming.

It's a watch. A Heuer with a brown face and gold numbers, on a black leather band. Jus doesn't know much about watches, but 10 he's about eighty-seven percent sure this one is vintage[2] and worth more money than Mama's ever had in her bank account at once. He carefully removes it and flips it over. The inside of the band is stamped with the letters EJR.

"My grandfather bought that watch in the 1940s," Mr. Julian says. 15 "His name, like Manny's, was Emmanuel Julian Rivers. It's been passed to the eldest male for two generations now. We want you to have it."

Jus is dumbfounded. "I, uhh . . . I don't know what to say."

"You don't have to say anything," Dr. Rivers says. "Just knowing 20 it's in your possession means a lot to us."

Jus looks back and forth between Dr. and Mr. Rivers, who are both smiling but obviously waiting for *some* kind of response from him.

His eyes drop to the watch. Which puts a big-ass[3] lump[4] in his throat. There's no talking past it, so he does the only other thing that 25 makes sense.

He stretches out[5] his wrist and puts it on.

---

1 in sb.'s stead (fml): when you take sb.'s place instead of them **2** vintage (adj): old but of high quality **3** big-ass (sl): enormous, huge **4** lump (n): solid and compact piece or mass **5** stretch out: hold out a part of your body straight

CHAPTER 17

The first thing Jus notices when he pulls into the visitor lot of the Fulton Regional Youth Detention Center is how much the building reminds him of a high school. It makes his stomach twist a little. Holding kids deemed[1] *menaces*[2] *to society* in a place that would be
5 completely normal if not for the twelve-foot barbed-wire-topped[3] fences seems like someone's bad idea of a joke. Like, *Oh, look at this nice-ass school... HA! GOTCHA! LOCKDOWN, FOOL!*

After Justyce puts the car in park, he takes a minute to look around. Let it sink in that he's really here. That he's about to go inside
10 a "juvie[4]" and sit down with the guy who killed Castillo, the cop who profiled Jus and started him on this failure of a "social experiment" trying to be like Martin.

He almost can't believe it.

Once Jus started at Bras Prep, Quan and those other guys became
15 nothing more than reminders of the life Jus wanted to escape. Quan never made fun of Jus the way the rest of them did, but still: hearing that Quan wanted to see him was a little suspect[5].

But then he couldn't stop thinking about it. Suspicion[6] finally gave way to curiosity[7], and here he is.

20 The minute he steps inside the facility[8], the guard by the door gives him a once-over before pointing toward an area marked VISITORS. Jus is smacked with a sweat-inducing[9] wave of discomfort[10].

---

1 deem sth. (fml): consider sth. in a particular way **2** menace ['menəs] to society: sb./sth. that is a risk for everybody else in a community **3** barbed-wired-topped: ending in sharp spikes at close intervals **4** juvie ['dʒuːvɪ] (sl) (AE): short for juvenile detention center, a prison for young people who have been found guilty of a crime **5** suspect (adj): cannot be trusted **6** suspicion: feeling that sb./sth. cannot be trusted **7** curiosity: strong interest in learning sth. **8** facility: building meant for a particular purpose **9** sweat-inducing: making you sweat **10** discomfort (n): unpleasant, uncomfortable feeling

He leaves his ID[1] and keys with the lady at check-in, and a second guard lifts his chin as Jus approaches the metal detector[2]. "Damn, boy," he says, taking in Justyce's button-down[3], pressed khakis, and loafers. "You cleaner than some of the lawyers that come up in here."

"Uhh . . . Thanks."   5

"Who you here to see?"

"Quan Banks."

The guard nods. "Go on through," he says. "Show those boys what they could be like if they got they shit together[4], ya hear me? She'll walk you down." He gestures to the check-in lady now waiting for   10
Justyce to step into the long hallway.

Jus follows her past a bunch of white-walled rooms—classrooms, they look like—until they reach a large steel door with a tall rectangular window that Jus suspects is bulletproof[5]. The room has maybe six or seven young guys in orange jumpsuits[6] inside with their visitors. As the lady punches[7] a code into the keypad on the door, Jus spots Quan waiting for him.   15

The door opens. Voices spill out[8] into the hallway. Quan lifts his head. He and Jus meet eyes. A smile spreads into Quan's cheeks, and as it overtakes his entire face, Jus remembers the last time he saw   20
it: the summer before fifth grade when Quan beat Jus at Monopoly for the first time. Seeing Quan smile like that makes Jus even more nervous about being here.

"Brainiac[9]!" Quan says, standing to greet Jus. "So glad you made it, homie!"   25

"Yeah." Jus peeks[10] over his shoulder at the now-shut exit door. "It's been a while."

"Have a seat, my nigga. Have a seat."

---

1 ID (n): identification **2** metal detector: device that signals when metal comes close to it **3** button-down (n): shirt that closes at the front with buttons **4** got they shit together (sl): have their things in order **5** bulletproof: bullets cannot pass through **6** jumpsuit: clothing made in one piece that covers the whole body, like overalls, workwear **7** punch sth. in/into: enter sth. on a keyboard **8** spill sth. (v): flow out **9** brainiac (infml) (AE): highly intelligent person **10** peek (v): look hastily and secretively

Quan sits back down, and Jus follows suit[1]. Seeing the other kids in the jumpsuits talking to their visitors makes Jus anxious[2] to leave. Especially since the majority of the guys in the room look like him.

5   It's depressing.

"So how you been, Justyce?" Quan asks.

Jus scratches his head. "Truthfully? I've seen better days, man."

"Real fucked up about Manny."

"Yeah. It is fucked up." Saying the words is like a weight lifting.
10 "One minute, we're ridin' along, and the next . . ." Jus sighs and shakes his head.

"What about you, homie? You recoverin'[3] all right and everything?"

"Well, my arm is workin' again, if that's what you mean."

15   "Yo, when I saw that cop's face on the news—" Quan stops talking. "Nah, never mind, never mind."

"What about him, man?"

Quan looks Jus in the eye. Then he leans closer, beckoning[4] Jus to follow suit. "You know that cop they say I popped[5]?"

20   How could Justyce forget? "Yeah. I do, actually."

"That asshole who opened fire on you and Manny? He was dude's partner."

Jus almost falls off the chair. "Castillo?" he says. "Tomás Castillo was Garrett Tison's *partner*?"

25   "Yup."

"How do you know that?"

"Tison was there the night I . . . uhh . . ."

"The night you shot Castillo."

"Allegedly."

30   Jus sits back in his chair to let it all sink in.

---

1 follow suit: do the same action as sb. after they have done it **2** anxious: (here) impatient, in a hurry to do sth. **3** recover (v): become healthy again after illness, injury, etc. **4** beckon ['bekən]: giving sb. a signal to follow or come closer
5 pop (sl): kill by shooting

"You good, dawg?" Quan says.

"Huh?"

"You lookin' a little shook[1] over there."

Should Jus tell him? Nothin' to lose, right?

Jus takes a quick peek around and leans forward. "Can I tell you   5
something crazy?"

"I'm listenin'."

"Well, like a week before you . . . before Castillo died, dude
arrested my ass. My girl was drunk, and I was tryna get her home,
but he thought I was carjacking her. Put me in cuffs and wouldn't   10
let me say a word."

"So the muthafucka got his just deserts[2]." Quan cracks his
knuckles.

Justyce takes in Quan's tough-guy[3] expression and orange jumpsuit as the power of his words, and seeming lack of remorse[4], settle   15
into Jus's bones.

Jus leans forward again. "Tell me why you did it, dawg."

Quan's features harden[5]. "Why I did what?"

"Quan, I know you confessed. You don't have to act innocent
with me."   20

"I don't know what you talkin' about, man." Quan crosses his
arms.

All right, then. Different approach. "Okay, new question: Why
would someone do what you're accused of doing?"

Quan shrugs. "If that's what someone's told to do, they do it."   25

"Who would tell someone to do that, though?"

Quan turns away and Jus can see he's about to lose him again.
But Jus really needs to know because now there's a new question
on the table: Who's to say Garrett Tison's quickness to pull the trigger[6] wasn't caused by seeing his partner killed by a black kid? It's   30

---

1 shook (sl) (AE): emotionally upset **2** just deserts: the punishment that sb.
deserves **3** tough-guy (adj): appearing strong and not easily hurt **4** remorse (n):
feeling of regret for sth. you have done **5** harden (v): become hard **6** pull the
trigger: shoot a gun

no excuse, of course. But Jus *knows* the effects of trauma are real: he watched his dad lash out[1] at his mom for years.

"Wait, forget that 'who would tell' question. I just really need to understand, Quan. I got shot and Manny's dead because Garrett
5 Tison thought *I* had a gun. Now you're tellin' me he was *there* when you kill—I mean, when his partner got shot?"

Quan's eyes narrow. "Whatchu trying to say, man?"

"I'm not trying to say anything, Quan. Just put yourself in my shoes. All of this shit is foreign to me."

10 For a minute, nobody says anything, and Jus is sure his coming here was a mistake. But then Quan starts talking. "Aiight, listen up: where I come from, resistance is existence, homie. Every day I woke up in my hood coulda been my last. You wanna survive? Get wit[2] some niggas who won't turn on you, and y'all do whatever it takes
15 to stay at the top, you feel me? My dudes . . . they're like family to me. They've got my back[3] as long as I have theirs. Somebody tells you to make a move, you make a move. No questions asked."

Jus shakes his head. "Not buyin' it[4], dawg. Don't forget I grew up right around the corner from you."

20 "Last I checked, *your* way got you capped[5] and Manny killed," Quan says.

Jus can't really respond to that.

"I know you all about gettin' ahead and everything, Justyce, but you gotta face reality at some point. These white people don't got no
25 respect for us, dawg. *Especially* the cops. All they 'protect and serve'[6] is their own interests. You just gon'[7] continue to bend ya knee[8] after they *proved* that shit by killin' ya best friend?"

Again, Jus has nothing.

"Can't even say I was surprised when I heard, man," Quan con-
30 tinues. "You and Manny were good dudes, and y'all *still* got a raw-ass

---

1 lash out at sb.: hit or kick sb. **2** wit (sl): with **3** have sb.'s back: support sb. unconditionally **4** buy sth. (sl): believe sth. **5** cap (sl): shoot sb./sth. **6** protect and serve: motto of the police in the US **7** gon' (sl): going to **8** bend your knee: obey, submit

deal[1]. That's why I wanted to see you. Talk. I got a counselor here, but I can't tell that white lady none of this shit. She won't get it."

Jus nods. "You know what, Quan? I feel you."

And he really does.

"It's fucked up—there's no escaping the BMC," Quan says.   5

"The BMC?"

"Yeah. Black Man's Curse[2]. World's got diarrhea[3] and dudes like us are the toilet."

"Guess that's one way to put it."

"Let me tell you when I learned: my second time in juvie, I was   10
fourteen. There was this seventeen-year-old rich white boy there, Shawn. Dude had got up in the middle of the night and stabbed his dad like eight times."

"Damn!"

"Right? They tried to get him on an attempted murder charge,   15
but homeboy's lawyer got some doctor to come in and say dude was sleepwalking[4]. And the shit worked! Judge dropped the charge down to simple assault. Guy got sixty days at a youth development campus[5], then got to go home."

"You serious?"   20

"Yup. Meanwhile, they locked my ass up for a year on a petty theft charge cuz it was my 'second offense.' Prosecutor actually referred to me as a 'career criminal' at the hearing[6]." Quan shakes his head. "I think that was prolly the moment I gave up. Why try to do right if people will always look at me and assume wrong?"   25

Justyce can't respond to that. He knows Quan committed actual crimes, whereas *his* only error was reaching to turn the music down, but Jus has to admit he's thought that same thing—what *is* the point in trying to do right?

---

1 raw-ass deal (infml): harsh treatment **2** curse (n): idea that a supernatural power put an evil and harmful spell on you **3** diarrhea [ˌdaɪəˈriːə] (AE): *Durchfall* **4** sleepwalking: walking and acting while still sleeping **5** youth development campus: centers that provide treatment and education to juveniles in order to prepare them for a fresh start **6** hearing (n): meeting in court or before a judge in which evidence is collected

"So what do I do, then, man?" he asks, surprising even himself with the question. "What's the alternative?" He swallows the next thought: *Winding up in jail doesn't seem like the way to go.*

Quan shrugs. "Well, as a wise man once told me, the solution is twofold[1]: first, you gotta use the power you already got, man. People fear dudes like us. When they fear you, they don't fuck with you, feel me?"

Jus doesn't feel Quan, but he nods anyway.

"Second, you need to get you a crew to roll with[2]. There's strength in numbers. Matter fact . . . You should give Martel a call," Quan goes on. "He's like a big brother to a lot of us. Taught us everything we know."

This makes Justyce's heart race. He knows exactly who Martel is and what he's about (hello, Black Jihad?). The last thing he wants is to get involved with some gang leader. "Nah, man, it's cool. I've learned plenty from you." He peeks over his shoulder at the exit again.

Quan grins. "I'ma give you Trey's number. He'll put you in touch with Martel."

"You really don't have to do that, Quan. I promise you, I'm all right."

"It's hard out there by yourself, man. Martel gets it." Quan looks Jus right in the eyes, and a stone drops into Jus's gut. "You'll be welcomed if you want in," he says.

"For real, dawg. I'm good. Besides, I don't have anything to write with."

"I'm sure you'll remember the number until you get back to your phone. You ready?"

As soon as Quan recites the last digit, a guard Jus failed to notice says, "Time's up!" The whole way back to his car, some of Quan's words run laps[3] in Jus's head: *Resistance is existence. . . . These white people don't got no respect for us. . . . There's no escaping the Black*

---

1 twofold (adj): consisting of two parts **2** a crew to roll with (infml): becoming part of a criminal gang **3** lap (n): one round on a racetrack

Man's Curse It's exactly the kind of thinking Jus tried to combat with the letters to Martin.

But asking *What would Martin do?* didn't help, did it? That's why he stopped writing them.

There's one thing Quan said that Jus can't dispute[1]: doing things Jus's way got him and his best friend shot. Yeah, Quan's in jail, but at least he's alive.

That's more than can be said for Manny.

Before sticking the key into the ignition, Jus grabs his cell phone from the center console. Before he can change his mind, he punches Trey's number in.

---

1 dispute (v): debate, discuss

CHAPTER 18

Turns out *not* using the number is harder than Jus anticipates[1],
especially when he's alone with nothing but memories of his homeboy. He's hanging out after school in Doc's classroom to avoid making the call a few days later when SJ busts through the door like she's
5 being chased by rabid[2] dogs.

The sight of her punches the air right out of Jus's lungs. They hav-
en't really talked since the funeral a couple of weeks ago, but seeing
her so . . . *SJ*? Well, it centers[3] him in a way he doesn't expect.

"You *guys*!"

10 "Yes, Sarah-Jane?" says Doc, the picture of calm.

"Do you have *any idea* what's going on right now?"

"Can't say we do," Doc replies.

"Where's your TV remote?"

Doc pulls the remote from his desk drawer and passes it to her.
15 Once the TV is on and tuned to the right channel, Jus finds it hard
to breathe for a different reason.

There on the screen, big and bold and bright and blatant, is a picture from Jared's Halloween-Political-Statement-
Turned-Brush-with-Death. Of course everyone else—Blake the
20 Klansman included—has been cropped out[4] of the version making
national news. It just shows Justyce McAllister as Thug Extraordi-
naire[5].

"We've heard about his grades, SAT scores, and admission to an
Ivy League school," the anchor[6] says, "but a picture speaks a thou-
25 sand words. This kid grew up in the same neighborhood as the

---

1 anticipate: expect, foresee **2** rabid: violent **3** center sb. (v): make sb. feel calm
4 crop out sth.: select a part of a photograph and remove it **5** Thug Extraordi-
naire: particular outstanding criminal **6** anchor: sb. who presents the news

young man accused of murdering Garrett Tison's partner more or less on a whim[1]."

"You gotta be kidding me," Jus says.

People all over the country have rallied[2] to the cause: wearing Justice for JAM T-shirts (JAM being Justyce and Manny) and riding with their music loud from 12:19 until 12:21 every Saturday afternoon to commemorate the time of the argument between them and Garrett. But if there's one thing Jus knows from the Shemar Carson and Tavarrius Jenkins cases, it really doesn't take more than a photo to sway[3] mass opinion.

SJ crosses her arms, and the three of them lean in to hear the "analysis" of some anti–gang violence pundit[4] who appears on a split screen with the anchor. "I mean it's obvious this kid was leading a double life," the guy is saying. "You know what they say, Steven: you can remove the kid from the thug life . . . But ya can't remove the thug life from the kid."

SJ: You son of a bitch.

Doc: Shhh . . .

SJ: This is blatant defamation[5] of character!

Pundit: There're all these reports about how great a kid Emmanuel Rivers was. But if *this* was the company he kept? Well, I really don't know, Steven.

Jus: [*Shakes his head.*] Unbelievable.

Steven: We've received some reports that this other young man you mentioned—Quan Banks—is a relative of Emmanuel Rivers. You know anything about that?

Pundit: It wouldn't surprise me if both boys had ties to Banks. Who's to say Officer Tison didn't see them on the scene the night his partner was murdered right before his eyes? You have to put the pieces together, Steven: Garrett Tison and Tommy Castillo respond to a complaint about loud music, there's a Range Rover parked in the

1 on a whim: based on a quick decision **2** rally (v): get together in mass protest for a cause **3** sway sb. (v): influence sb. **4** pundit: expert **5** defamation: lying about sb. to hurt their reputation

driveway of the offending domicile[1], and some thug kid pops out of the backseat with a shotgun. Now that we're learning about all these connections, who's to say it wasn't the same Range Rover Emmanuel Rivers was driving? Officer Tison says these boys pointed a gun
5 at him, and after seeing this picture, I can't say I'd put it past[2] them.

As the news cuts to another segment, SJ turns the television off.

Doc looks too furious to speak. All Jus can do is put his head in his hands.

"Effing Jared," SJ says. "If that cretin[3] wouldn't've—"
10 SJ's phone rings, and Jus lifts his head. When she sees the screen, her eyebrows jump to the ceiling.

"Who is it?" Jus says.

SJ holds out the phone. *Douche-Nugget* is the name displayed. "Speak of the spawn of Satan[4] and he shall make his presence
15 known."

"Jared?" Jus asks.

"Yep. I'll take it in the hallway."

As she pulls the door closed, Jus hears her yell: *"SEEN THE NEWS TODAY, ASSHOLE?"*
20 Doc throws an arm around Jus's shoulder and gives him a shake. "Wanna talk about it?"

"This is some bullshit, Doc!" Jus kicks the desk beside him and it topples onto its side.

"Yep." Doc rights it.
25 "Is it not enough that Manny's *dead,* man? It's like these people *want* Garrett to get away with it." Jus shakes his head. "I *knew* I shoulda said no to Jared's idea. Definitely shouldn't've let him take that picture . . . But I ignored how I was feelin' about it because I was tryna be like—" He grits[5] his teeth.
30 "Like Martin?"

Jus nods.

---

1 domicile: home **2** not put it past sb.: believing that sb. is able to do sth. wrong **3** cretin ['kriːtn] (infml, offensive): idiot **4** spawn of Satan (derog): son of the devil **5** grit your teeth: clenching your teeth because of anger and frustration

"You still writing your letters?"

"Nah, man."

"Why not?"

Jus shrugs. "Don't see the point. My 'experiment' obviously didn't work. Don't wanna think about it anymore."   5

"I see."

"You know what's crazy, Doc?"

"What's that?"

"I've got one memory of the day everything happened: sharp[1] pains in my chest and shoulder, and then not being able to breathe.   10 In *that* moment when I thought I was dying, it hit me: despite how good of a dude Martin was, they still killed him, man."

Doc nods. "I know. But I don't think knowing he'd be killed would've changed the way he lived, Jus. He challenged the status quo[2] and helped bring about some change. Pretty sure that was his   15 goal. Wouldn't you agree?"

"All I know is he and Manny are dead, and *I'm* being cast[3] as the bad guy."

"I get that. Look, Jus, people need the craziness in the world to make some sort of sense to them. That idiot 'pundit' would rather   20 believe you and Manny were thugs than believe a twenty-year vet-eran cop made a snap judgment based on skin color. He identifies with the cop. If the cop is capable of murder, it means he's capable of the same. He can't accept that."

"Well, that's *his* hangup[4]. Shouldn't be my problem." "You're   25 right. But it *is* your problem because you're affected[5] by it. I know it's shitty, excuse my language, and it's definitely not fair. But these people have to justify Garrett's actions. They *need* to believe you're a bad guy who got what he deserved in order for their world to keep spinning the way it always has."   30

"How does that help *me*, Doc?"

---

1 sharp (adj): intense **2** status quo: the current political and social situation
3 cast (v): assign a role **4** hang up (infml): mental block **5** be affected by sth.: be influenced by sth.

"It doesn't."

Jus shakes his head again. Trey's number flashes through his mind. "So why even try to be 'good'?"

"You can't change how other people think and act, but you're in
5 full control of *you*. When it comes down to it, the only question that matters is this: If nothing in the world ever changes, what type of man are *you* gonna be?"

A dense[1] silence settles over the room, but just as Jus is about to speak again, SJ comes back in. For a minute, she just stands with her
10 back against the doorframe and her eyebrows furrowed.

"SJ?" Doc says. "Everything all right?"

She snaps out of the daze. "Assclown Christensen seems to be shedding[2] his douchey skin, you guys."

"Huh?" from Jus.

15 SJ comes over and drops down in the empty seat next to him. She turns to look at him. Right in his eyes. "He wants to clear this up[3]," she says.

"Wait." Jus shakes his head. "Back up. I'm confused."

"Jared. That was him on the phone."

20 "Got that part."

"Well, he's pissed about what they did with the Halloween picture. Says his dad is calling some people so they'll show the entire shot, Blake's Klan idiocy[4] included."

Jus doesn't know what to say. Isn't this the same guy who was
25 about to press charges against Manny for the beatdown[5] he got? Why the hell is he being Mr. Noble[6] all of a sudden? "What do you think is up with him?"

---

1 dense: heavy **2** shed your douchey skin (infml): fundamentally rethink your offensive position **3** clear sth up: set sth. right that was a misunderstanding **4** idiocy ['ɪdiəsi]: very stupid behavior, stupidity **5** beatdown (infml) (AE): beating **6** Mr. Noble (infml): sb. who is not selfish and morally good

"I honestly couldn't tell you. He seemed a little ... disillusioned[1]? Like I picked up the phone and called him an asshole, and it sounded like he just kind of crumpled[2].

'I can't even disagree with you, SJ,' he said. 'This is all my fault.' I had to look at my phone to check who I was talking to."   5

Jus's jaw clenches. "So now he wants to be the Great White Hope[3]—"

"Correct me if I'm wrong," Doc interrupts, "but Manny and Jared were good friends, right?"

Jus shrugs. "Yeah, I guess."   10

"It occur to either of you that maybe the guy doesn't want his friend's name dragged through the mud[4] any more than you do?"

Neither SJ nor Jus responds.

"Cut Jared some slack[5]. He's grieving too."

Jus's eyes drift across the room to where Manny and Jared used   15
to sit side by side in Socio Evo. "Yeah, okay, Doc."

"I need to hit the men's room." Doc stands. "Excuse me." When Doc leaves, Jus's awareness of SJ's presence kicks up a notch[6]. He looks at her hands on the desk and sees that her nails are painted green. It makes him smile: during one of their tournament prep   20
sessions at her house, they'd taken a break to make a snack run to the local drugstore. Just before they checked out, SJ asked Jus what his favorite color was. When he told her green, she ran off and came back with the bottle of nail polish. Justyce clears his throat. "So—"

"Wait, I need to say something."   25

"Okay."

She turns to face him. "I owe you an apology. For ... bailing[7]." She picks at her nails. "After the tournament. With no explanation. I'm sorry."

---

1 disillusioned: disappointed **2** crumple (v): break down **3** The Great White Hope: play written by Howard Sackler in 1967 that deals with racism **4** drag sth. through mud: damage the reputation of sb./sth. **5** cut sb. some slack (sl) (AE): be easier on sb. **6** notch (n): degree **7** bail (v) (AE): leave sb. in a situation without saying goodbye

"Oh." Some emotion he doesn't recognize surges in his chest. He's on dangerous ground and he knows it. Especially considering the way she's looking at him. "You, uhh . . . mind explaining now?"

"I panicked?"

5   "You panicked."

"Well, there was Melo . . . and I didn't know where you stood with her or how I fit? Anyway. Point is, it won't happen again."

"Okay."

"I mean it, Jus. I want to be here for you. Anything you need. A
10   friend, a hug, whatever."

"Thanks, S." Jus bumps her with his shoulder. "I really appreciate it."

She nods. "So we're good?"

"Yeah." Jus smiles. "We're good."

VP RELEASED FOR RABBLE-ROUSING[1]!

By: Sonya Kitress
For The Tribune

Julian Rivers, executive vice president of Davidson Wells Financial Corporation, has stepped down from his position [5] following troubling reports of his involvement in the Justice for JAM movement. According to CEO[2] Chuck Wallace, photographs of Mr. Rivers on the front lines of an Atlanta march that shut down traffic for hours last week triggered[3] the loss of several high-profile[4] clients and approximately[5] [10] $80 million in revenue[6] for the asset management firm. In a press release[7] yesterday afternoon, Wallace stated: "While we respect the gravity[8] of the tragic loss of a child, involvement in publicly disruptive[9] activity is grounds for investigation[10] and potential[11] dismissal[12]. Mr. Rivers has been a [15] tremendous[13] asset at Davidson Wells for well over nineteen years, and while we hate to see him go, we've mutually[14] agreed to part ways."

Rivers's son, Emmanuel, was killed in a shooting during a dispute over loud music in late January. A trial date for the shooter, who was indicted last month, has not yet been set. [20]

---

1 rabble-rousing: the activity of making speeches to crowds of people intending to make them angry or excited, especially for political aims **2** CEO: chief executive officer; boss of a company **3** trigger sth.: cause sth. to happen **4** high-profile: very important **5** approximately: roughly **6** revenue: money that comes into a company **7** press release: official statement of a company or institution on an issue given to the press **8** gravity: seriousness **9** disruptive: trouble-making **10** investigation: act of examining sb./sth. **11** potential: possible **12** dismissal: act of firing sb. from their job **13** tremendous: very good/important **14** mutually: do sth. or make a decision together with sb.

CHAPTER 19

There's not a whole lot Jus is sure of these days, but he knows he shouldn't be in this seat at the back of the number 87 bus right now. If it weren't for the newspaper article in his pocket, he'd be studying for finals or hanging out with SJ. But all he's thought about over the
5 past few days is how sad Manny's parents were when they invited him over to tell him they were moving.

Doc gave Jus a copy of the article about Mr. Julian "stepping down[1]" the morning it was released. His first thought: instead of Sonya Kitress, the name on the article should be *Nunya Bidness*[2].
10 Manny's parents more or less sponsored the Atlanta chapter of the Justice for JAM movement, so of course they'd participated in the local marches. It wasn't their fault the one they were photographed at overflowed[3] onto the highway, blocking all northbound[4] *and* southbound[5] lanes.

15 The day the Riverses shared their relocation plans, they   also told Jus that Mr. Julian had received an ultimatum[6]. Basically: *Sever all ties with that so-called movement or clear out of that corner office*[7] (in so many words). Mr. Julian told Jus he "calmly explained the meaning of *civil disobedience*[8]" before removing his framed degrees[9]
20 from the wall.

Jus is on the number 87 bus, the final bus in the commute from Oak Ridge to Wynwood Heights, because what Quan said—*there's no escaping the Black Man's Curse*—has been echoing in his head since he left the Riverses' house. He has no idea where else to go or

---

1 step down: leave an office or position **2** Nunya Bidness (sl) (AE): none of your business **3** overflow (v): spill over **4** northbound: heading north **5** southbound: heading south **6** ultimatum: warning to sb. to act within a time limit or face consequences **7** corner office: office given to important people in a company **8** civil disobedience: form of protest where you peacefully refuse to follow certain laws **9** degree: academic qualifications

who else to turn to. SJ's great, but not for this, and while he *could* go to Doc, Jus doesn't really want to hear any more *stay good even though the world craps on you* advice.

Mama would throttle[1] Jus if she knew where he was going— *everybody* in the neighborhood knows who Martel is—but frankly, she hasn't been any help lately either: every time he calls or stops by, she brings up SJ.

All Jus knows is he's got this shitty feeling in his gut, kind of like somebody crawled into his stomach and ran a cheese grater[2] over the inside. He needs to get rid of it somehow. Talk to somebody who *gets* what he's feeling because they've felt it too.

You know who gets it? Deuce Diggs. Jus has been listening to his music a lot since he woke up without a best friend. There's one track he's had on repeat since the article dropped:

Turn on the news, another black man slain[3].
They say "It's okay. Save your voice, don't complain.
This isn't about race, so stop using that excuse.
Now look at this funny picture of Obama in a noose[4]!
See how color-blind we are? You're not really black to me.
Underneath, where it matters, we both bleed red, you see?
So put away that race card; it ain't 1962.
There's no more segregation[5] . . . isn't that enough for you?"

But of course Jus doesn't have access to Deuce Diggs; he can't just call him up and say: *Hey, dawg, I'm feelin' what you're feelin'. Can we talk?*

Jus remembers what Quan said about the neighborhood guys being "like family." That Martel would *get it.* That he'd be welcomed if he wanted in.

---

1 throttle sb.: choke sb. **2** cheese grater: *Käsereibe* **3** slay sb./sth. (v): kill sb./ sth. violently **4** noose: rope that has a circular loop at the end that is used to hang people **5** racial segregation: separating people by their race in everyday life

That's really why he's on this bus right now: he's sick of feeling alone.

The first thing to cross Jus's mind as he steps off the bus is the irony of looking for solace[1] in the place he was anxious to get away from. As someone drives by in a brand-new Benz, he also feels a twinge[2] of guilt over refusing to drive his new car to Martel's house. How can he be mad at white people for profiling when he's doing the same damn thing they do? *Lock your doors . . . Hide your valuables . . .* He even left Manny's watch at home.

This is the shit that has to be remedied[3].

He hangs a left onto Wynwood Street and spots the gunmetal Range Rover Trey said would be in the driveway. Despite it being an older model than the one Manny drove, seeing it makes Jus want to make a run for it.

He should turn back. He really should. Turn back, and go "home" to his mahogany desk and school-issued Mac-Book.

But he doesn't.

It's not until Jus starts up the driveway that he notices the three guys sitting on the porch. Trey is there, plus White Boy Brad and the dude who had the gun during the Halloween disaster.

"Oho! If it isn't Smarty-Pants!" Brad says.

The gun-toter[4]—Jus doesn't remember his name—smiles. " 'Sup, Justyce?" he says. "Great to see ya, buddy, 'ol pal[5]!"

The others laugh.

Jus's eyes immediately drop to the guy's waistband. He can see the bulge[6] of the gun handle[7] beneath dude's shirt. It gives him a chill.

He tries to pull himself together. " 'Sup, y'all?"

They all laugh again.

---

1 solace [ˈsɑːləs] (n): comfort **2** twinge [twɪndʒ] (n): a sudden short feeling of pain **3** remedy (v): set straight, correct **4** gun-toter (infml): gun-carrying person **5** 'ol pal: old pal, old friend **6** bulge (n): bump **7** gun-handle: part of a gun where you hold it

Trey gives Jus the same kind of once-over he did at the Halloween party all those months ago. He smiles that sneery[1] creeper smile[2], and Jus feels like his guts are about to make an appearance inside his boxer-briefs[3]. Trey shouts: "Hey, Martel, you got company," over his shoulder at the screen door, and the second Jus steps onto ⁵ the porch, a voice calls out from inside: "Come on in, young brotha!"

Even though his heart is about to explode, Jus pulls the door open and enters the house he's only ever eyed warily[4] due to rumors[5] about all the drugs and guns hidden inside. He follows a short hallway lined with what appear to be African relics[6]: tribal[7] masks, ¹⁰ framed hieroglyphics[8], and a silhouette painting of Nefertiti—he can tell by the cylindrical headpiece[9] that reminds him of the flattop haircuts some of the NBA players are trying to bring back.

There's similar art all over the walls of the living room. Jus is sure this house could win the world record for largest collection ¹⁵ of ancient Egyptian paraphernalia[10]. His gaze roams[11] the space until it lands on a youngish, bearded black man in a dashiki[12] shirt and kufi[13] hat. He's sitting cross-legged in a papasan chair[14] with a kente-cloth[15] cushion. Most notable is the black tracking device[16] strapped to his ankle—so *this* is why dude couldn't meet Jus at a ²⁰ coffee shop.

"Welcome," the guy says. "You must be Justyce."

"Yep . . . That's me."

"Martel." He sticks out a hand, and Jus walks over to shake it. "Pleasure to meet you." ²⁵

---

1 sneery: scornful **2** creeper smile: scary looking smile **3** boxer-briefs: underpants **4** warily: cautiously **5** rumor: story that people tell but cannot be verified **6** relic: historical object **7** tribal (adj): belonging to a traditional community **8** hieroglyph [ˈhaɪərəɡlɪf]: ancient Egyptian symbolic writing **9** headpiece: ornament worn on the head **10** paraphernalia [ˌpærəfərˈneɪliə]: large collection of things or equipment connected to a particular activity **11** roam (v): wander **12** dashiki [dæˈʃiːki]: loose-fitting shirt or tunic originating from West Africa **13** kufi [kuːfˈiː]: round cap originating from West Africa and worn by Muslim men **14** papasan chair: large bowl-like chair **15** kente-cloth [ˈkɛntɪ klɒθ]: Ghanaian cloth made of brightly coloured strips of cloth **16** tracking device: used by the police to track people who are placed under house arrest

"Likewise[1]." Jus looks around again and then sticks his hands in his pockets.

Though Jus has known of the Black Jihad leader since middle school, Martel in person is *not* what he expected. He honestly has
5 no idea what to say to the guy. The silence is beginning to morph[2] into something straight-up menacing[3]. "Cool art."

Martel smiles. "I like to surround myself with reminders of ancient Kemet[4] so the boys and I never forget our imperial[5] roots. You know anything about that?"

10 Jus shrugs. "I've studied it a bit, but I don't know a whole lot. Sorry."

"No need to apologize." Martel tents[6] his fingers beneath his chin. "You'll learn, young brotha. You'll learn. The Europeans succeeded in denigrating[7] and enslaving[8] peoples of African descent,
15 but there's royal blood flowing through your veins, you hear me?"

Justyce nods and swallows. "Yes, sir."

"People across the diaspora[9] have been treated as inferior for so long, most of us have habituated to the lie of white superiority[10]. But never forget," Martel goes on, "your ancestors survived a transatlan-
20 tic[11] journey, built this nation from the ground up, and maintained a semblance of humanity, even when the very conditions of their existence suggested they were less than human. 'Jihad' is the act of striving[12], persevering[13]. *That* is your legacy, young brotha. This country belongs to *you*."

25 As Jus listens to Martel's voice, he can feel himself relaxing. He doesn't know if it's the voice itself, or what it's saying, or the art, or

---

1 likewise: the same to you **2** morph (v): change form and character **3** menace sb./sth. ['menəs] (v): threaten sb./sth., be a possible danger to sth./sb. **4** Kemet: ancient name of Egypt **5** imperial (adj): royal **6** tent (v): put your fingers together in order to form a tent shape **7** denigrate sb./sth. ['denɪɡreɪt]: belittle, criticize sb./sth. unfairly **8** enslave: to sell into slavery **9** diaspora [daɪ'æspərə]: people who had to leave their homeland **10** superiority [suːˌpɪri'ɔːrəti]: behaviour that shows that you think you are better than other people **11** transatlantic: across the Atlantic ocean **12** strive to (v): try hard (to) **13** persevere: carry on even when it gets difficult

the incense[1], or the atmosphere, but something about Martel and his house makes Jus feel looser than he's felt in a while.

He looks at Martel—who's been watching him, reading him, studying him, he can tell, ever since he stepped into the room—and . . . yeah. Martel *does* get it. Quan said Jus would be welcomed, and 5 that's exactly how he feels. The disarming[2] effect gives him vertigo[3].

"So what can I do for you, Justyce?" Martel asks. Before he knows it, Jus is telling Martel all the stuff he can't talk to anyone else about: how it felt to be profiled, the Martin experiment and how it failed, how alone he's felt and how furious he is, how much he misses his 10 homeboy.

Martel listens intently[4], stroking his beard, lowering his eyes when Jus gets to Manny's death, narrowing them when he hears about Mr. Julian's job. By the time Jus finishes getting it all out, he's sprawled[5] on his back across the giant ankh[6] at the center of Mar- 15 tel's Egyptian rug. He feels empty . . . in a good way.

Martel gets up without a word and disappears into what must be the kitchen. Jus lets his head fall to the left. That's when he sees the sawed-off[7] shotgun tucked beneath the edge of the coffee table.

It smacks him like a battering ram[8]: he shouldn't be here. No 20 matter how chill Martel seems, the dude is a criminal (Hello? House arrest anklet[9]?). Those guys outside . . . they're the same ones who threatened to *shoot* Manny's old friends.

What the hell is Jus *doing* here?

There's a tap on his foot, so Jus looks up. Martel is squatting 25 beside him with a glass in his hand.

---

1 incense (n): sweet smelling substance when burned **2** disarming: (here) charming **3** vertigo: dizziness **4** intently: with strong attention and interest **5** sprawl (v): lie with legs and arms spread out **6** ankh [ɑːŋk]: ancient Egyptian symbol of life that looks like a cross with a loop on top **7** sawed-off shotgun (AE): shotgun that has been cut short to make it easier to carry and hide **8** battering ram: heavy object used to break down a door **9** house arrest anklet: device worn around an ankle that prevents the person from leaving his or her house

Jus sits up and takes a drink. The first gulp is too big—he doesn't know why he didn't expect the thing to be alcoholic. He coughs as what feels like the flames of hell run down his esophagus[1] through his chest and into his stomach.

5   Martel laughs. Jus can tell it's a laugh of delighted amusement. It makes sense that the neighborhood guys without dads flock to Martel. "So, the illusion wore off, huh? Seeing some truth now?" he says.

Jus nods, and that feeling of defeat returns to his chest now that the fire from the liquor is gone.

10   "You ready to strike back?"

Justyce knew this question would come. What he isn't ready for, though, is the fear that seems to have elbowed its way in front of his fury. *Is* he ready to strike back? It's definitely not what Manny would want.

15   But the reason he's even *here* is because Manny is gone.

Justyce looks up at Martel. There's no anxiety in this dude's face. No pressure. No fear. Jus lifts his glass to his lips again—

Trey bursts into the room with Gun Guy and White Boy Brad on his heels. "Yo, check this out," he says, passing a cell phone to Martel.
20 They all crowd around.

"Brad, that's the fool you punched at that Halloween party, right? With the KKK shit on?" Gun Guy asks.

"Yep," Brad says. "That's him."

"Homeboy says you whupped[2] his ass a few months ago, Justyce."
25 Martel hands Jus the phone.

There, in big, bold letters above a picture of Blake Benson: *JUSTYCE McALLISTER'S VIOLENT PAST: A FORMER VICTIM SPEAKS OUT.*

"Damn, Smarty-Pants," Trey says, shaking Jus's shoulder. "Didn't
30 know you had it in you!"

"Hell yeah, bruh!" from Gun Guy. "You scrap[3] like this dude say you do, you can roll with us anytime."

---

1 esophagus [iˈsɑːfəgəs] (AE): *Speiseröhre* **2** whup sb. (AE) (infml): beat sb. up
3 scrap (v): fight

"For real. You more like us than I realized!" Brad says.

That does it for Justyce. "I gotta go." He scrambles to his feet and makes a break for the door, refusing to turn around when they call out after him.

"Let him go," he hears from Martel on the way out.   5

CHAPTER 20

Mrs. Friedman looks so shocked to see Justyce standing on her doorstep, he peeks over his shoulder to make sure there's not a ghost or
something behind him.

"Justyce?"

5   "Hey, Mrs. F. Is Sarah-Jane home?"

"Sure. Come in, come in."

As Mrs. F stands there with her eyes popping out of her head,
Jus thinks maybe he shouldn't have just shown up with no notice.
Not that he made a conscious decision to do that . . . He got back to

10 school from Martel's, hopped[1] in his car, and let his instincts[2] lead.

This is where he ended up.

"I should've called," he says. "I'm sorry—"

"No, no, that's not it at all, I'm just—Well, we've really missed you
around here."

15   They *missed* him?

"SJ's up in her room, but do you mind saying hello to Neil? He'll
be thrilled[3] to see you."

"Uhh . . . sure."

Mrs. F leads him around to the living room where Mr. Friedman

20 is kicked back in his recliner[4] watching reruns of the Final Four.
"Neil, look who's here," she says.

When Mr. Friedman sees Jus, he sits bolt upright[5]. "Jusmeister!"

"Hey, Mr. F."

"It's really you!" Mr. Friedman jumps up to hug Jus, who winces a

25 little from the pressure on his shoulder. "How are you? We're so glad
to see you, son!"

"I can see that."

---

1 hop in (infml): get into a car **2** instinct (n): natural feeling **3** thrilled: excited
4 recliner: armchair that tilts backwards **5** bolt upright: sit up very straight

The Friedmans laugh.

Jus swallows. It's a little overwhelming, all this . . . love.

"Sarah's in her room if you want to head up, Justyce," Mrs. F says.

"Thank you. And thanks for the warm welcome. Promise I'll call first next time."   5

"Oh, don't be silly."

Jus smiles and turns to head upstairs.

"Hey, Jusmeister, if you need *anything*—anything at all, I mean it—don't hesitate[1] to call us, all right?" Mr. F says from behind him.

At first, Jus recoils[2]. If there's one thing he *can't* handle right now,   10
it's pity.

But as he looks over his shoulder into the faces of SJ's parents, he knows this is different.

He clears his throat. "Thanks so much, sir. That really means a lot to me."   15

"You betcha[3], kiddo[4]."

"Okay, we've embarrassed ourselves enough," Mrs. F says. "Go on up."

As Jus climbs, he gets nervous. What if SJ isn't as cool with him dropping in as her parents were? What if she's busy? What if she's   20
asleep? What is he even going to say to her?

The door is cracked, and he can hear what sounds like NPR[5] and Carrie Underwood playing simultaneously inside SJ's room.

Typical.

He knocks.   25

"Come in."

She's stretched out on the bed in her Bras Prep lacrosse shorts and a T-shirt, with an open calculus[6] book in her lap. When she sees it's him, she sits up just like her dad did, wearing the same expression her mom had.   30

---

1 hesitate: wait or stop before doing sth. because you are unsure **2** recoil (v): move back away from sth./sb. because of a feeling of disgust **3** betcha (infml): bet you **4** kiddo (infml): used when you affectionately address sb. younger
5 NPR: National Public Radio **6** calculus: advanced mathematics

It makes him smile. "Hey," he says.

"Hey! Uhh . . ." She scrambles around for a second like she can't figure out what to do. Shuts the calc book, sets it aside, and swings her legs around so she's sitting on the edge of the bed. "Oh!" She
5   grabs a remote from the nightstand and points it at the speakers attached to her computer on the desk. NPR and Carrie go quiet. "So . . . You're, uhh . . . you're here."

Jus laughs. "That's what your parents said."

"Oh god, did they totally attack you? I'm so sorry." She shakes
10 her head. "You're literally *all* they talk about these days. I would've warned you if I'd known you were coming."

Jus laughs again. "It's all good. Actually felt pretty nice."

She smiles. "Wanna sit?" Points to the empty space beside her.

He sits so close that their shoulders and legs are touching. She's
15 warm.

"So . . . what brings you to la casa¹ de Friedman, Mr. McAllister?" She nudges his knee with her own.

He turns to look at her. "You."

"Me?"

20 "Yeah, I . . . umm . . ." He looks away. "Well—"

"Everything okay, Jus?" She touches his forearm just past his wrist, and the memory of handcuffs overwhelms him even all these months later.

His eyes drop to her hands, and he feels a weight slip off his
25 shoulders. They're chipped² now, but her nails are still painted his favorite color.

Jus stands, pulls SJ up, and wraps her in a hug that lifts her off her feet.

"Umm . . . okay," she says.

30 He inhales a whiff³ of her fruity shampoo. "I almost joined a gang today," he says.

"Huh?"

---

1 casa: Spanish for home **2** chipped: damaged at the edges because small pieces have broken off **3** whiff (n): brief smell

"I almost joined a gang." He puts her down. "Remember the guys I told you about from the Halloween party?"

"You mean the ones who threatened to *shoot* you?"

"Yeah. I went to see their leader."

"You *what*?"   5

"I was thinkin' about, uhhh . . . well, joining their crew."

She just gapes at him.

They both sit back on the bed, and he tells her about visiting Quan in juvie, and the sequence of events that led him to Martel's doorstep. At some point he starts crying. Which he'd normally   10
be embarrassed about. But he's not because it's the best he's felt since . . . well, since before he can remember.

Granted, part of feeling so good probably has to do with being wrapped in SJ's arms with his head on her shoulder. Jus has no idea when that happened, but here they are.   15

He can imagine Manny calling him a punk for letting her hold him while he cries like a big-ass baby, but instead of making him sad, the thought makes him smile—he can also imagine Manny saying *Took you long enough, fool.*

After a few minutes of silence, SJ lets him go, and he sits up.   20
"Thanks for that." He smiles at her.

She doesn't smile back.

"You okay?"

"Justyce, do you like me?"

"Huh?"   25

SJ clasps her hands in her lap. "Like . . . I know you're going through a lot right now . . ."

"But?" he says.

She looks at him. "I can't keep doing this to myself, Jus."

"What are you talking about, S?"   30

She sighs. "Okay, this is the thing: I've had a crush[1] on you since tenth grade."

"For real?"

---

1 crush (n) (infml): feeling love for sb. you do not have a relationship with

"Yes. At first, that's all it was, didn't expect anything to come of it. But then last semester, we started talking more and spending more time together, and it like . . . *evolved.*"

Jus doesn't know what to say.

5   "Problem is, I don't really know how to read you. Sometimes it seems like you're into[1] me, but other times you're kinda withdrawn[2]. Sometimes you look at me in a way that makes me wanna put the world on a platter[3] and hand it to you, but other times, you won't look at me at all."

10   "Damn, S."

"As much as I enjoy your friendship and company, I can't keep giving myself over to this hope we'll become something more. I need to know where you stand. So tell me the truth." She looks him right in the eye. "Do you like me, Jus?"

15   He gulps. "Uhh . . . I, uhh . . ."

"Oh my god. You totally don't."

"Huh? I didn't sa—"

"You hesitated!"

Jus peers down at his brown hands and sees Manny's watch.

20   "You know what? It's fine," she says. "We can still be frien—"

"S, I like you."

She glares at him. "Don't just say it to shut me up, Justyce."

"I'm not! I *do* like you, I swear! More than I've ever liked *any* girl."

"Why do I feel like there's a 'but'?"

25   He sighs.

"Melo, right?" she says.

"What? No! Melo and I are *done.* As in never-gonna-happen-again."

"So what is it? Is it me?"

30   "No! It's . . ." He looks around the room. Anywhere but at her. "It's complicated."

She drops her chin. "Just forget it."

---

1 be into sb. (infml): have feelings for sb. 2 withdrawn (adj): introverted
3 to hand sth. to sb. on a platter: give sth. valuable to sb. very easily

"Wait! No!"

It's now or never, dawg, Manny says in his head.

Jus turns to face her fully. "S, I'm sorry. For confusing you. You're right. I never said how I felt cuz I was scared to."

She fiddles[1] with her hands and doesn't respond.   5

Jus takes a deep breath. "This is the thing," he says. "My mom . . . Well, she's not real *keen* on me, uhh . . . dating girls who aren't African American."

SJ draws back. And then her head cocks[2] to one side. *"Really?"*

"Yup. It's been since I was little, but she's gotten more adamant   10
about it since—" He cuts off.

"Since the shooting," SJ says.

"Yeah."

She sighs.

"But I don't care anymore," Jus says.   15

"Huh?"

"About what she thinks. I don't care."

SJ lifts an eyebrow and crosses her arms. "And I'm the Easter Bunny."

Jus laughs. "Okay, I *care* but . . ." Jus takes in her face. Sees what   20
he'd be passing up. "I can't let it stop me," he says. "Life is too short."

She bites her lip. It drives Jus absolutely crazy.

"Let me make it clear right now," he says. "I *like* you, Sarah-Jane. No matter my mom's opinion, you mean a lot to me, and if you'll have me, I'd love to take you out sometime."   25

Her eyes narrow.

"Like on a date."

"I *know,* numbnuts." She rolls her eyes. And smiles. "You've never called me Sarah-Jane before."

He grins.   30

She blushes.

"Can't lie: it's *real* fun making your cheeks all red," he says.

---

1 fiddle with sth. (v) (infml): play with sth. in a nervous or restless manner
2 cock sth (v): tilt sth. to one direction

"Shut up!" She punches him.

It makes him laugh *and* want to kiss her. "So? What's up? We doin' this?"

She covers her face. "Will you *stop* making me blush[1]!"

5   "Nope."

"Ugh!" She huffs[2] and drops her hands. "You're all in?"

"I'm *all* in, girl."

Her eyes narrow for a second, and then: "Okay." She smiles again. Jus shakes his head. "Had to make me sweat for it, huh?"

10   "Just returning the favor."

"Touché."

A beat passes, and then: "Can I tell you something?" she says.

"You mean there's *more*?"

"Shut up. This is serious."

15   "Okay . . ." And now he's nervous.

She takes a *really* deep breath and shifts her gaze across the room. "Seeing you with all those tubes[3] in your body was probably the lowest moment of my life, Jus. To think I spent all that time being stupid, then almost lost you?" She shakes her head.

20   "I felt the same way when I saw you at the funeral."

Silence.

Then: "Justyce?"

"Yes, Sarah-Jane?"

"Can we agree not to be that stupid again?"

25   He smiles and drapes an arm around her shoulders. "Sounds like a plan to me."

---

1 blush: become red in the face because you are embarrassed or ashamed
2 huff (v): blow out air loudly **3** tube: long, hollow pipe made of metal, plastic, rubber, etc., through which liquids or gases move from one place to another

Transcript from nightly news, May 21

Anchor: Good evening, and welcome to the Channel 2 Nightly News.

In our top story tonight, investigators say a fire at the home of former Atlanta Police officer Garrett Tison was deliberately[1] set.

Investigator: Arson[2] was our initial suspicion due to the number of threatening phone calls and letters Mrs. Tison has received during her husband's detainment. We're now able to confirm that this fire was started from the outside.

(Cuts to picture of house's charred[3] remains.)

Anchor (v.o.): Police have apprehended[4] three teenage boys who were seen in the area on the night of the incident. Beverly Tison, Garrett's wife, sustained multiple second-degree burns[5], leaving her in serious condition.

Anchor (cont.): Tison's trial in connection with the January shooting that left one teenager dead and another wounded is set to begin approximately five weeks from today.

More on this story as it continues to develop.

---

1 deliberately: intentionally **2** arson [ˈɑːrsn]: crime of deliberately setting sth. on fire **3** charred: burnt **4** apprehend sb.: arrest sb. **5** second-degree burns: burns that are painful but usu. not life-threatening

CHAPTER 21

For the most part, Jus isn't surprised when a pair of cops approach him and Mama after Bras Prep's commencement ceremony. Since Blake's "Justyce assaulted me" stunt fell flat[1]—even the pundits were smart enough to ignore a kid photographed in a KKK robe—Jus fig-
5 ured it was only a matter of time before he got accused of something else.

And he was right: not twelve hours after news broke that the fire at Garrett Tison's house was set by someone outside it, the same newspeople who instigated[2] "Thug-Gate" were speculating about
10 Justyce's "involvement in the arson plot." Despite having nothing to do with it, for four days now, he's been waiting for someone—cop, reporter, angry mob[3]—to come after him.

Just sucks that he's still in his cap and gown[4], surrounded by his classmates and their families, when someone does.

15 "Justyce McAllister?" the female of the pair says. She's black. Slacks[5] and a button-down. Badge on her belt.

"Yes?"

"I'm Detective Rosalyn Douglass, and this is Officer Troy." She points to the white guy in uniform. "You mind if we ask you a few
20 questions?"

Mama steps forward and crosses her arms. "I'm his mother, and he's a minor[6]. What can I do for you, Officers?"

"We mean your son no harm, ma'am," says Officer Troy. "Just have a few queri—"

25 "I don't give my consent[7]."

---

1 fall flat: fail, be unsuccessful **2** instigate sth.: cause sth. usu. bad to begin, trigger sth. **3** mob (n): aggressive crowd of people **4** cap and gown: official clothes worn at an academic graduation ceremony **5** slacks: long pants **6** minor (n): underage person that is legally still a child **7** consent (n): permission

Detective: Ma'am, your son is seventeen years of age, and therefore an adult according to Georgia criminal law—

"My son isn't a criminal, so that law doesn't apply to him."

The detective sighs and looks around before taking a step forward and lowering her voice. "Ma'am, we know this is a big day for your son. We're trying not to make a scene here. If he's willing to cooperate and answer a few questions for us, we might be able to avoid this going any further than it has to."

"So lemme guess," Mama says. "You're good cop, and whitey over there is bad?"

"Ma, *stop*," Jus says. "Let's just hear them out so we can lea—"

"Do you officers have any idea of the kinda hell my boy's been through at the hands of people like you? He's been falsely accused and *unlawfully*[1] held under arrest. He's lost his best friend. He's been *shot*—"

Detective: We're well aware of your son's background, Ms. McAllister. Our goal is to make this as painless as possible.

Jus: What's this about?

Mama: I did *not* say you could talk to these people, Justyce!

Jus: Ma, if they wanna treat me like an adult, I'm gonna act like one.

She doesn't say anything.

Jus steps around her and looks each cop in the eye. "You were saying, Officers?"

The detective nods as the white cop pulls out a notepad. "We appreciate your cooperation, Mr. McAllister."

Justyce almost laughs.

Detective: On the night of May twentieth, there was a fire at the home of Garrett and Beverly Tison. The blaze was started at around eleven-forty-five p.m. You know anything about that?

Jus shrugs. "Only what I've seen on the news."

---

1 unlawfully: illegally

The detective's eyes narrow, and Justyce wonders if he's being too nonchalant[1]. He's telling the truth, of course, but they obviously don't know that.

Detective Douglass examines Justyce's face—which makes him
5 feel like a cockroach under a magnifying glass[2]. "Will you excuse us for a moment?" she says, gesturing[3] to the officer.

"Sure."

The moment they step away, Mama rounds[4] on Jus. "I don't appreciate you speaking to me that way in front of those police offi-
10 cers. You should've let me handle it."

"No offense, but I don't think this is somethin' you could 'handle,' Mama."

"Well, if you woulda kept your mouth shut—"

"You realize once they said I don't need your consent, refusing to
15 talk would've made it look like I had something to hide, right? I turn eighteen in three weeks and head to college in ten. You can't protect me forever."

Mama's jaw drops, but before she has a chance to respond, the cops come back.

20 "Okay, Justyce," the detective says. (So he's *Justyce* now, huh?) "This is the deal: we arrested three young men caught on camera siphoning[5] gasoline[6] from cars in a Walmart parking lot near the Tison home. Two of them . . ." Officer Troy passes her the notepad.

"'. . . Trey Filly and Bradley Mathers,'" she reads, "named you as an
25 accomplice."

Jus shakes his head. Of *course* it was Black Jihad. Jus can't *believe* he considered joining up with those fools. "I promise I had nothing to do with it, Detective."

---

1 nonchalant [ˌnɑːnʃəˈlɑːnt]: calm and unconcerned **2** magnifying glass: glass that makes things appear bigger than in real life **3** gesture sb. (v) [ˈdʒestʃər]: expressing an idea by movement of your hands and body **4** round on sb.: aggressively and suddenly criticize sb. **5** siphon sth. [ˈsaɪfn] (v): transfer liquid by using a tube **6** gasoline (AE): fuel

She nods. "Well, we're hesitant to believe these guys. For one, they've both tried to implicate[1] innocent parties before. For two, the third young man did *not* mention you, which, considering the circumstances, is a little odd."

"Okay . . ."   5

"I'm going to ask you a series of yes-or-no questions. Just answer truthfully and this should go pretty fast."

Jus nods.

"Were you aware of an arson plot involving the home of Garrett Tison?"   10

"No."

"Have you had any contact with Trey Filly or Bradley Mathers in the past two months?"

"Yes."

Mama gasps—Jus is sure she knows both of those clowns by   15 name—and the cops exchange another glance.

"How many times have you had contact with either of these boys in the past two months?"

"Once."

"And what was the nature of this contact?"   20

Justyce gulps. "I went to meet someone, and they were there."

"Who were you meeting?"

"If they're not connected to the arson, does it matter?" Mama cuts in.

The detective clears her throat. Jus is so relieved, he could kiss   25 Mama.

Detective Douglass continues: "Did you have any contact with either Trey Filly or Bradley Mathers on the night of May twentieth?"

"Absolutely not. Haven't seen or spoken to either of those guys since April twentieth."   30

Officer Troy's eyebrows rise. "That's pretty specific." "It was a pretty memorable[2] day."

---

1 implicate: say that sb. was involved in a crime **2** memorable: unforgettable because of being special

"What was memorable about it?" Detective Douglass asks.

"Something unrelated to what we're talking about."

Jus can feel Mama's gaze burning into him.

"Where were you on the night of May twentieth?" the detective goes on.

"I can assure you, it wasn't anywhere near those guys or that fire."

"Is there someone who can verify your whereabouts?"

"Ye—"

"I can," Mama says. "He was with me."

Jus could leave it at that. He knows he could. Yes, he can tell the cops are suspicious, but he knows that to dig deeper, they would need a warrant[1].

But lying to the police after everything he's been through?

Nah.

"You're getting confused, Ma. I wasn't with you. We went to visit Daddy's grave on the twenty-first, not the twentieth." And this is true.

"But—"

"On May twentieth, I was at my girlfriend's house. We were celebrating her parents' twentieth wedding anniversary."

Mama says nothing.

"I see," Detective Douglass says. "Would your girlfriend happen to be around here to verify[2] that?"

Justyce looks past her and the officer at the parting crowd.

"She would," he says. "She and her mom are headed right this way."

Mama doesn't say a word the entire trip home. When they pull into the driveway and she tries to get out, Justyce reaches over and pulls her door shut.

He locks it.

---

1 warrant (n): legal document that authorizes usu. the police to do sth.
2 verify sth: confirm that sth. is true or accurate

"Oh, so you holdin' me hostage[1] now?"

"You have somethin' you wanna say to me, Ma?"

"I certainly don't."

"You sure about that?"

"I don't have *anything* to say to you, Justyce."   5

"Well, *I* have some things to say to you—"

"That's funny. I've learned more about my son in the past two hours than I've known in four years, and *now* he wants to talk to me?"

"Mama—"   10

"Tell me somethin' . . . did you *ever* plan to let your mama know about this 'girlfriend' of yours?"

"Ma—"

"I can under*stand* you not wantin' to bring up your recent contact with the neighborhood gangbangers[2], but if you actually *care* 15 about this girl, seems to me like you would've at least *mention*—"

"You know why I didn't tell you anything, Mama!" She doesn't respond.

"I'm not saying keeping it from you was the right thing to do. But I *knew* no matter how happy I was, you woulda had somethin' neg- 20 ative to say. You reacted in the parking lot by frownin' at Mr. Friedman's hand like it was diseased!"

"I'm not shakin' no white man's hand, Justyce. Not after what that other one did to you."

"But what does that *solve*, Mama? Mr. Friedman and Garrett 25 Tison are totally different people."

Mama crosses her arms and turns to the window.

Jus shakes his head. "All my life, you've pushed me to be and do my absolute best. That's what SJ brings out of me, Ma. She makes me better."   30

"Don't you sit over there and tell yourself that lie, Justyce."

"It's not a lie!"

---

1 hold sb. hostage: *jdn. als Geisel halten* **2** gangbanger (AE): member of a criminal gang

"It certainly is. I taught you a long time ago, only person can 'make you better' is *you*."

Justyce grips the steering wheel. "Mama, if not for her, I don't know that I woulda made it through this school year. For ten months
5 now, people have been trying to tear[1] me down. SJ worked harder than *anybody* to make sure I stayed standing."

"Hmph."

"Whether you believe it or not, she brings out the best in me. When I'm with her, I *want* to overcome[2] everything." "I get what
10 you're saying, son, but there are plenty of brilliant black women who can do the same—"

Jus sighs. She doesn't get it at all.

"Ma, SJ is *Jewish*," he says. Manny said it to *him,* and it's a valid[3] point, isn't it? "I know you have issues with white folks, but her peo-
15 ple have been through hardship too."

"Doesn't matter, son. You can't see Jewish in her skin color. You tried to *help* that other girl and wound up in handcuffs. And her daddy is black, ain't he? If it looks white, it's white in this world."

"But it's not that *simple*—"
20 "Yeah it is. You just refuse to accept it. I sent you to that school so you'd have a chance at the best education. But with this foolish-ness[4] you've got in your head now, I'm wonderin' if that was such a good idea."

"So what you're saying is after a lifetime of getting picked apart
25 because of my skin color, I should dismiss the girl I love because of hers?"

Mama turns. "Love? Boy, you seventeen years old. You don't know nothin' about *love*."

"You were eighteen when you married Daddy—"
30 "And look where it got me."

---

1 tear sb. down (infml) (AE): criticize sb. harshly 2 overcome: master
3 valid: reasonable 4 foolishness: stupidity

Jus leans back against the headrest[1] and shuts his eyes. For a minute, neither of them says anything.

Then Mama sniffles.

"Aww, Ma! Don't *cry*—"

"I'm afraid, son. This world is hard enough for a boy like you with-   5
out the extra obstacles[2]. That man almost *killed* you, Justyce! And
what for? What were you doing wrong? Listenin' to some music he
didn't like?"

Jus doesn't respond.

He can't.   10

"I know you think I'm being unreasonable, but I—I can't give you
my blessing on this one," she says. "I know you grown and you gonna
do what you want, but you on your own here, baby."

"Come on, Ma—"

"As you made clear earlier, I can't protect you forever, right?"   15
She unlocks her door and gets out of the car.

---

1 headrest: back of a seat that supports your head **2** obstacle: sth. that stops
you doing sth. or makes it slower, more difficult

CHAPTER 22

Sitting on the witness stand[1], Jus *wishes* he could go back to the days when all he had to worry about was his mama not liking his girlfriend. The DA's[2]—Mr. Rentzen's—questioning is running pretty smooth, and Mama, Doc, the Riverses, and the Friedmans are all
5 there in the gallery to support him. But testifying[3] with his best friend's murderer glowering[4] at him from twenty feet away? It's the hardest thing he's ever had to do.

By the time Mr. Rentzen finishes his questions, the court has heard the tragic tale[5] of two college-bound[6] African American boys,
10 gunned down at a traffic light by an angry white man who used a racial slur[7] and fired his weapon at them when they didn't comply with his demands.

Jus, with tears in his eyes, recounts the final minutes of Manny's life, and for a second he's tempted to relax, especially when Doc
15 gives him a thumbs-up from where he's sitting.

But then the defense attorney[8], a short white lady with blond hair and an upturned[9] nose, steps up to the podium[10]. She and Jus lock eyes.

He can tell she's out for blood.

20 "Mr. McAllister," she begins, all cool, calm, and collected[11]. "Isn't it true that at the beginning of your story, you stated that you and Emmanuel Rivers were 'just driving around'?"

---

1 witness stand: place where people stand or sit to give evidence in court
2 DA (AE): district attorney, state lawyer who puts people on trial accused of crimes 3 testify: witness giving a detailed account of a situation after promising to tell the truth 4 glower (v): look at sb. with an angry expression 5 tale: story
6 college-bound: sb. who plans to go to college 7 racial slur: racist insult
8 defense attorney [dɪ'fens ə'tɜːni]: lawyer that defends a person in court charged with a crime 9 upturned: pointing upwards 10 podium: platform 11 calm, cool, and collected: relaxed and sure about what you are doing

"It is."

"That's not what you originally intended to do, though, is it?"

"I'm not sure I understand the question," Jus says.

"When Mr. Rivers retrieved[1] you from your dormitory on January twenty-sixth, you had no idea you were getting into his car for the sake of 'driving around,' did you?"

"No."

"So there were other plans, then."

Jus gulps. "Yes, there were."

"What were they?"

"We were supposed to go hiking."

"But you *didn't* go hiking, did you?"

"No."

"Emmanuel Rivers didn't really feel *up* to hiking anymore, is that correct?"

"Uhh . . ."

"Let me remind you that you are under oath, Mr. McAllister."

Jus clears his throat. "No. Manny didn't feel up to hiking."

"Did he mention why?"

"He did."

"He'd gotten a phone call that morning, correct?"

"Yes, he had."

"And you're aware of what that phone call was about?" Jus sighs and drops his head. "I am."

"I'm sorry, it's difficult to hear you when you don't speak into the microphone. Can you repeat that?"

"I said I *am.*"

"You are *what*, Mr. McAllister?"

---

1 retrieve sb.: get sb.

"I'm aware of what the phone call was about."

"Enlighten[1] us if you will, please."

Jus looks at Mr. Rivers, who has his jaw clenched so tight, it wouldn't surprise Jus if his teeth were cracking.

5 "He'd gotten a phone call from his friend's father," Jus says.

"That's a bit vague[2]. I'm sure you can be more specific. What could this 'friend's' father have mentioned that would've been so distressing to Mr. Rivers, he'd no longer feel up to hiking?"

Jus clenches *his* teeth. "A disagreement."

10 "A 'disagreement' involving whom?"

"Manny and the friend."

"Interesting." She shuffles her papers on the podium. "Your Honor[3], I'd like to enter into evidence a police report, filed on January twenty-sixth, that alleges[4] Emmanuel Rivers physically *attacked*
15 a Mr. Jared Christensen on Monday, January twenty-first."

Mr. Rivers is shooting eye-daggers[5] at the attorney.

"It wasn't like that," Jus says.

The attorney's eyebrows rise. "Oh, it wasn't?"

"No."

20 "Which part of the report is incorrect?"

"Manny didn't attack Jared."

"So you were there to witness this 'disagreement'?"

Jus drops his head again. "No."

"We can't hear you, Mr. McAlliste—"

25 "I said no."

"So you can't be completely sure Mr. Rivers didn't attack Mr. Christensen."

"Manny wasn't that type of guy."

"What type of guy?"

---

1 enlighten sb.: inform sb. **2** vague: not clear **3** Your Honor: respectful title used when talking to a judge **4** allege [əˈledʒ]: claim sth. as a fact but without having proof **5** eye-dagger: when you give sb. an aggressive look

"The type who 'attacks' people unprovoked[1]."

"So you're suggesting there was provocation[2]."

"Yes. There was."

"What makes you so sure?"

"Because Manny told me . . ."

Jus sees SJ close her eyes, and he realizes his mistake.

"I mean—"

"So Mr. Rivers *did,* in fact, inform you that he'd assaulted Jared Christensen?"

Jus doesn't respond.

"Mr. McAllister?" Justyce just stares at her.

"Your Honor?"

"Answer the question, Mr. McAllister," the judge says.

Justyce clears his throat. "Yes. Manny told me Jared made an inappropriate[3] joke, so he hit him."

"Who hit whom?"

"Manny hit Jared."

"Hmm." The attorney nods. "Sounds like a fairly *familiar* set of circumstances, doesn't it, Mr. McAllister?"

"Objection[4]," Mr. Rentzen says. "The question is ambiguous[5]."

"Sustained[6]," says the judge.

"I'll rephrase[7]," she says. "You were involved in a similar altercation[8] on the night of January eighteenth, correct?"

"You'll have to be more specific," Jus says.

The attorney doesn't miss a beat. "I have a statement here from a Mr. Blake Benson alleging that you assaulted him *and* Jared Christensen, unprovoked, at Mr. Benson's home the night of January eighteenth."

---

1 unprovoked: happening without any cause or justification **2** provocation: sb.'s action or speech that is the reason for sb. to act aggressively **3** inappropriate: in bad taste, offensive **4** objection: a formal challenge to sth. in court **5** ambiguous [æmˈbɪɡjuəs]: unclear and confusing because there is not one interpretation of it **6** sustained: when a judge accepts a lawyer's complaint **7** rephrase: reformulate **8** altercation [ˌɔːltərˈkeɪʃn]: heated and angry disagreement

SJ bites her lip.

"Do you deny this accusation, Mr. McAllister?"

"It wasn't unprovoked."

"Are you saying you *didn't* assault Blake Benson at his own birth-
5 day party?"

"No . . ."

"So you *did* assault Blake Benson and Jared Christensen."

"Well, yes, but I was provoked."

She actually smiles. "You arrived at Blake Benson's house with
10 Emmanuel Rivers, and within ten minutes, you'd started an argument with Mr. Benson, correct?"

"I didn't start the argument. He did."

She looks down at the podium. "It says here that Mr. Benson
asked you and Mr. Rivers to come meet a young lady he was inter-
15 ested in. Is this true?"

"No."

"Oh, it's not?"

"He wasn't 'interested' in her. He just wanted to get her in bed."

"Mr. Benson said those exact words?"

20 "No . . . but he implied."

"I see, so the young lady was a friend of yours, and you were
defending her honor, then?"

"I didn't know the girl, but—"

"You were jealous, then."

25 "What? No!"

"For *whatever* reason, you didn't like that Blake Benson wanted
to take this girl to bed. So you assaulted him?"

"That's not how it happened."

"Ah, that's right. Jared Christensen came over to defend Blake
30 Benson, whom you were threatening at his own birthday party, and
so you assaulted both of them."

"That's not what happened!"

"Maintain your composure, Mr. McAllister," the judge says.

Jus breathes in deep and looks at SJ. She nods.

"Tell me something," the lawyer says. "After you attacked Jared Christensen and Blake Benson, Emmanuel Rivers reprimanded[1] *you*, correct? He sided with the victims of your unprovoked assault—"

"I already told you I didn't attack them."

"Well, you certainly didn't wish Mr. Benson a *happy* birthday, did you?"

"Some words were exchanged that led to an altercation."

"Can you be more specific, Mr. McAllister?"

Jus looks at Garrett. "A lot has happened since then. Can't say I remember very clearly."

"Hmm . . . are you having difficulty remembering due to more recent events, or because you were illegally intoxicated[2]?"

"Objection, Your Honor!" says Mr. Rentzen.

"Overruled[3]."

"Had you been drinking on the night of January eighteenth, Mr. McAllister?" she presses.

Jus sighs. "Yes, I had."

"And you hit Jared Christensen *and* Blake Benson, correct?"

"They were making racist comments—"

"A simple yes or no will do."

Jus can feel Mama's gaze. "Yes."

The defense attorney nods. "Mr. McAllister, now that we've established that both you *and* Mr. Rivers had a history of responding violently to perceived[4] verbal slights[5], let's return to January twenty-sixth of this year. How familiar are you with the City of Atlanta Code of Ordinances?"

"Not very."

"Your Honor, I would like to enter the following into evidence." She pulls a sheet of paper from her stack and walks over to the witness stand. "Mr. McAllister, read Article Four, section seventy-four-

---

1 reprimand (v): tell sb. clearly that they are doing sth. wrong or bad **2** intoxicated: under the influence of alcohol or drugs **3** overruled: when a judge rejects a lawyer's complaint **4** perceive: judge sth. as sth., but maybe based on your perspective and not on fact **5** slights: insults

dash-one-thirty-three, aloud[1] for the court, please. It's highlighted there for you."

Jus looks into the crowd. Mama and Mrs. Friedman *both* seem on the verge[2] of hopping[3] the rail[4] and smacking[5] Garrett's attorney.

5 He reads: " 'Above certain levels, noise or noise disturbance is detrimental[6] to the health and welfare of the citizenry[7] and the individual's right to peaceful and quiet enjoyment. Therefore, it is hereby declared to be the policy of the city to prohibit[8] noise distur-bances[9] from all sources.' "

10 "Would you say your loud music was in violation of this ordi-nance[10], Mr. McAllister?"

"What does this have to do with your client *shooting* me and my best friend?"

"Judge, please advise the witness that I am the one asking the 15 questions."

Now even Doc looks pissed.

"Watch your tone, Mr. McAllister," the judge says.

"My client is an officer of the law, Mr. McAllister. By refusing to lower the volume of your music, you were in direct opposition to a 20 police order."

"We didn't know he was a police officer. He didn't show us a badge—"

"And yet the ordinance clearly states that noise disturbance vio-lates the rights of others to peace and quiet. But of course you and 25 your friend couldn't have cared less about anyone *else's* rights, could you?"

---

1 read sth. aloud: loudly read sth. to an audience **2** on the verge: when you about to do sth. **3** hop (v): jump **4** rail: horizontal bar separating the audience in a court room from the jury, judge, lawyer, etc. **5** smack sb./sth. (AE): to hit someone with your open hand **6** detrimental: harmful **7** citizenry [ˈsɪtɪzənri]: all the people living in a town, city, country **8** prohibit sth.: forbid sth.
9 noise disturbance: loud music, shouting or unpleasant noise **10** ordinance: law issued by a city authority

Jus doesn't respond.

"Mr. McAllister, did your friend, Emmanuel Rivers, turn the music *up* when he was asked to turn it down?"

"Yes."

"Did the music you were listening to contain the line *Here comes* 5 *the fun . . . wait for the sound of the gun*?"

"Yes, but that's out of contex[1]—"

"Did Mr. Rivers use foul language[2] and make an obscene[3] gesture toward my client that *you* would've perceived as threat?"

"I don't know what your client thought. I'm not him." 10

"Are you aware that my client witnessed the shooting death of his partner by a young man physically similar to yourself?"

"That doesn't have anything to do with me—"

"Oh, but it does," she says. "Because you had contact with this young man back in March, didn't you?" 15

Jus sighs. Dr. Rivers shuts her eyes and shakes her head. "Yes, I did, but—"

"And that young man—Quan Banks, I believe his name is— connected you to a group of young men with extensive criminal records and known gang affiliations[4], yes?" 20

"Yes, but—"

"And you met with these young men shortly before they deliberately set my client's house on fire, is that correct?"

"It is, but I didn't have anything to do with that—"

"No further questions, Your Honor." 25

---

1 out of context: without providing the surrounding words **2** foul language: use of swear/curse words **3** obscene [əbˈsiːn]: connected with sex in a way that most people find offensive **4** affiliation: connection with sb./sth.

Garrett Tison: MURDERER?

THE JURY IS STILL OUT
By: Ariel Trejetty

Yesterday morning, a Georgia jury found former Atlanta
5 police officer Garrett Tison guilty on three of the four charges
related to the January incident in which he was accused of
shooting two teenage boys after an argument over the volume of music.

After 27 hours of deliberation[1], Tison was convicted[2] of
two misdemeanors—disorderly[3] conduct[4] and discharge[5] of
10 a pistol near a public highway—and aggravated assault[6], the
less severe of the two felonies. The jury was unable to reach
a consensus[7] regarding the felony murder charge, and a mistrial[8] was declared on that count.

Tison testified that he feared for his life, citing[9] 27 years
15 of law enforcement[10] experience in support of his ability to
detect a genuine threat. Though Tison's claim that the teens
had a gun was unsupported by evidence, the surviving teen,
Justyce McAllister's, exposed connection to known gang
members, including sixteen-year-old Quan Banks, the young
20 man charged with murdering Tison's partner last August,
cast a considerable pall[11] over the proceedings.

Mr. Tison will be retried[12] on the murder count[13] and sen-
tenced[14] on all convictions at a later date.

---

1 deliberation: thorough consideration and discussion **2** convicted of sth.:
found guilty of a criminal offense by a judge **3** disorderly: lawless **4** conduct:
behaviour **5** discharge (n): act of shootin a gun **6** aggravated assault: illegal act
in which a person attacks sb. violently **7** consensus: agreement **8** mistrial
['mɪstraɪəl] (AE): trial in which the jury cannot find an agreement **9** cite (v):
putting sth. forward in order to support your argument **10** law enforcement:
police **11** cast a pall over sth.: create an unpleasant atmosphere **12** retry (v): try
a case in court for a second time **13** murder count: charging sb. with murder
14 sentence sb.: declare a punishment

CHAPTER 23

It's been two days.

Two full days, and the words *unable to reach a verdict*[1] and *mistrial* and *later date* are still bouncing around in Jus's head.

He and SJ have been watching National Geographic pretty much nonstop since they got back from the announcement of the verdict, but every time he blinks[2], Jus sees the third juror from the right in the back row, eyeing him like *he* shoulda been on trial for murder.

A hung jury[3].

No verdict.

No sentence.

Another trial.

SJ sighs like she can read Jus's mind. She's stretched out on the couch with her head in his lap, looking at a documentary about the migration of monarch butterflies, but Jus doubts she's actually watching. Nothing in the world frustrates Sarah-Jane Friedman more than a "miscarriage of justice[4]."

It's all so messed up. In two weeks, he and this gorgeous girl are supposed to get into his car and drive up the East Coast together. They're supposed to go to Yale first and get Jus set up in the dorms—Mama wanted to come, but she can't get off work, so it'll be just the two of them. Once Jus is in, they're supposed to take the train from New Haven to New York, where they'll meet Mr. and Mrs. Friedman and get SJ settled at Columbia.

They're supposed to be moving on. Starting the next chapter. Never looking back.

---

1 verdict: judgement made by the jury or judge **2** blink (v): close and open your eyes quickly **3** hung jury: jury that cannot decide on a verdict **4** miscarriage of justice [ˌmɪskærɪdʒ əv ˈdʒʌstɪs] (fml): when a court fails to make the right decision and innocent people suffer

But at some point in the next six months, he's going to have to come back here. He's going to have to relive[1] the afternoon he got shot and lost Manny.

Again.

5 "What are you thinking about?" SJ says.

He could tell her, but from the bags[2] under her eyes, she's got enough on her mind. "Just the fact that you're the best thing in my life," he says.

"Oh god, Jus. Rom-com[3] much? Le barf[4]."

10 He laughs, and she smiles, and for a moment, everything's fine.

Course it doesn't last.

"Jus, I think I hate everything," she says. "Why can't we all get along like butterflies?"

He tucks her hair behind her ear. Tries to shift his focus to the TV, 15 where layer upon layer of monarchs cover the trees in some Mexican forest. While he appreciates her sentiment, Jus wonders if she notices that all *those* butterflies look exactly alike.

His cell phone rings. It's Mr. Rentzen.

He declines[5] the call. The longer he can go without having to 20 speak to the DA, the better.

Now all he can think about is how exhausted Mr. Rivers seemed as they said goodbye outside the courtroom. As much as *Jus* hates that the death of his best friend was minimized by the hung jury, he can't begin to imagine what Manny's parents must be going 25 through.

Voice mail notification chimes.

Then a text message: "Justyce, call me ASAP[6]."

Jus erases it.

The phone rings again.

30 "Who *is* that?" SJ asks.

---

1 relive: experiencing an unpleasant memory again by remembering it vividly
2 bags: draping skin under your eyes   **3** romcom (infml): romantic comedy
4 le barf (sl): catchphrase to indicate your disgust   **5** decline sth.: not accepting
sth. (e.g. a telephone call)   **6** asap: as soon as possible

"It's Rentzen." Jus declines the second call.

"Oh god," SJ says. "Can we change your number?"

Mrs. F comes in from the kitchen with a phone to her ear.

"Justyce, Mr. Rentzen is trying to get ahold of you—What's that?" she says into the phone. Her eyes go wide. "You can't be serious, Jeff." 5

That can't be good.

SJ sits up. "Mom? What's the matter?"

Mrs. F holds up her index finger[1] and continues to speak into the phone: "Mmhmm . . . Oh good lord . . . This is . . . And the perpetrators[2]? . . . I can't believe this, Jeff . . ." 10

Justyce can't breathe. He lets his head fall back against the couch and closes his eyes.

"Mom, can you take it to another room?" SJ says, putting her hand on Justyce's knee. "You're gonna give Jus a frickin'[3] heart attack!"

"Jeff, I'll call you back. I need to talk to the kids. . . . 15

Yeah . . . Strictly confidential[4], I understand."

Things can't get worse, *can they?*

Mrs. F hangs up.

"Mom?" from SJ.

"There won't be a second trial," Mrs. F says. 20

Jus rockets[5] up, and SJ grabs his hand. *"What?"*

Mrs. F looks at the phone in her hand. Then at the two of them.

"Garrett Tison is dead."

---

1 index finger: finger next to the thumb **2** perpetrator: person who commits a crime **3** fricking (adj) (sl): an inoffensive synonym for 'fucking' **4** confidential: secret **5** rocket (v): rise up quickly

Transcript from morning news, August 9

Good morning, and welcome to *Rise 'N' Shine*[1] *Atlanta* on Fox 4.

In our top story this morning, a mere[2] forty-eight hours after a mistrial was declared in the proceedings against him, former APD officer Garrett Tison was found dead inside his cell at the Clarke County Jail.

While details about the incident are being withheld pending investigation, three men have been implicated in the matter, two of whom were already awaiting trial on murder charges.

In a statement to police, Garrett Tison's attorney claimed she received a phone call from Mr. Tison alleging that guards refused to put him in isolation despite his complaints about receiving threats.

The sheriff's office is also conducting an internal administrative review.

More on this story as it continues to develop.

---

1 rise and shine (infml): wake up, originally name of a radio program **2** mere: used to show how short, small, unimportant, etc. sth. is

August 25

DEAR MARTIN,

Welp, I'm here.

The illustrious[1] Yale University.

I'm actually writing this from beneath a picture of you that SJ hung over my desk. It was a going-away gift[2] from Doc.

I gotta be honest, Martin: your picture is making me a little uncomfortable.

Actually, no. I take that back. It's not your picture. It's being here at this school.

A lot has happened since I last wrote to you, most of which I haven't really had time to process. Hard to believe that this time last year, I was starting my whole experiment.

What I find most interesting reading through the letters: I can't figure out what I was trying to accomplish[3]. Yeah, I wanted to "be like Martin," but to what end? I wasn't trying to move mountains of injustice or fight for the equal rights of masses of people . . .

So what exactly was I trying to achieve? I've been thinking about it for days and haven't come up with an answer.

On the one hand, I feel like I should thank you: while there were black students at Yale as early as the 1850s, I doubt I would be here without all you did to "challenge the status quo," as Doc put it.

On the other hand, though, I feel crazy outta place. I'm in a four-person suite broken down into a living room and two bedrooms, and while I was in here setting up my half of the room, my roommate came in looking like he stepped straight out of a Ralph Lauren[4] ad. Blond, blue-eyed white dude with a deep side part and comb-over[5], wearing a blindingly

---

1 illustrious [ɪˈlʌstriəs]: very famous and much admired **2** going-away gift: present you get when you move away **3** accomplish: achieve **4** Ralph Lauren: expensive fashion brand **5** comb-over: a strip of hair combed over a hairless patch on a man's head in an attempt to hide it

white polo tucked into plaid shorts, and a pair of tasseled loafers. After staring at your picture for a few seconds, and then giving me the type of once-over that would've made the guys from my neighborhood throw a punch, dude finally stuck out his hand. "Roosevelt Carothers," he said.

5   Now, okay, Martin. I tried not to judge the magazine by the advertising[1], but standing there with this guy looking down his pointy[2] nose at me made me wish I were rooming with Jared Christensen (he's going to school here too). At least then I would've known what I was dealing with.

10   But this Roosevelt guy?

"So where you from . . . is it Just-ICE? Like rhymes with 'price'?"

Martin . . .

"It's Justice, man. Just with a 'y.' I'm from Atlanta."

Everything went downhill[3] from there because he put two and two
15   together—my name and face were all over the news until like a week ago. Then when SJ came back in from the bathroom and I introduced her as my girlfriend, dude's entire demeanor[4] changed for the negative. I know I wasn't imagining it because as soon as he left, SJ said, "What the hell is his deal?"

20   Martin, I just—It never ends, does it? No matter what I do, for the rest of my life I'm gonna find myself in situations like this, aren't I? It's exactly what Mr. Julian told Manny and me, but there's a part of me that still doesn't wanna believe it.

And all right, benefit of the doubt[5]: maybe I'm making this a race
25   thing when it's not. I'll admit my filter's a little tainted[6] after the past eight months . . . scratch that: after the past year.

But that's the thing, Martin. I CAN'T not notice when someone is eyeing me like I'm less than[7], and at this point, my mind automatically goes to race.

---

1 not to a judge a magazine by the advertisement: phrase that indicates that you should not judge sb. by his/her outward appearance **2** pointy: sharp end
3 downhill: continuously getting worse **4** demeanor [dɪˈmiːnər] (AE): behavior
5 the benefit of the doubt: believing in sth. as long as the opposite has not been proven **6** my filter's a little tainted: my perceptions are negatively influenced
7 less than: of lesser importance

No clue what to do about that.

Which brings me back to my original point: What was my goal with the Be Like Martin thing? Was I trying to get more respect? (Fail.) Was I trying to be "more acceptable"? (Fail.) Did I think it would keep me out of trouble? (Epic[1] fail.) Really, what was the purpose?

What I do know: I just went from being one of three black students in a class of 82 to one of . . . well, very, very few in a much larger number. Yeah, Garrett Tison is gone, but like Mr. Julian said, the world is full of people who will always see me as inferior[2]. Roomie Roosevelt just proved that.

I keep coming back to something Doc said during "Thug-Gate": If nothing ever changes, what type of man am I gonna be? Chewing[3] on that over the past few days, I've started to wonder if maybe my experiment failed because I was asking the wrong damn question.

Every challenge I've faced, it's been What would Martin do? and I could never come up with a real answer. But if I go with Doc's thinking—Who would Martin BE?—well, that's easy: you'd be yourself. THE eminent[4] MLK: nonviolent, not easily discouraged, and firm in your beliefs.

And maybe that's my problem: I haven't really figured out who I am or what I believe yet.

I found this letter you wrote the editor of the Atlanta Constitution where you said, "We (as in Black people) want and are entitled to the basic rights and opportunities of American citizens . . ." It's from 1946, which means you were seventeen when you wrote it. That's the same age I was when I had that exact thought for the first time.

Not sure if you were the Martin the world is familiar with by seventeen (prolly not, right?), but knowing you were my age gives me hope that maybe I've got some time to figure things out.

---

1 epic: monumental **2** inferior: lower in status **3** chew on sth.: reflect on sth. thoroughly **4** eminent: great

At least I hope I do. If not, this is gonna be a long four years. Hell, a long rest of my life.

Anyway, I gotta run. SJ and I have a train to catch. Thanks for everything.

> Until we meet again,
> Justyce

FOUR MONTHS LATER

There's already someone standing over Manny's grave as Justyce approaches. Part of him wants to turn around, go sit in his car until the person leaves—but he knows that's not what Manny would want him to do.

5   " 'Sup, dawg?" Jus says as he steps up.

EMMANUEL JULIAN RIVERS
BELOVED SON
"YOU HAVE SORROW NOW, BUT I WILL SEE YOU AGAIN,
AND YOUR HEARTS WILL REJOICE."

10   Jared looks at Justyce, and then back at the headstone[1]. He wipes his eyes. "How's it goin', man?" "Sorry for interrupting," Jus says.

"It's cool. Kinda nice to have someone else here. Merry Christmas, by the way."

"Same to you."

15   Jared exhales. It fogs up the air in front of his face. "I still miss him *so* much, dude," he says, his voice breaking. "It's been almost a year and I *still* just can't—I'm sorry, man, you don't wanna hear all this."

"Nah, it's cool." Now Jus's eyes are moist. "I understand, man. I really do."

20   "He's never gonna visit me at college or be my best man[2], you know?" Jared shakes his head. "When I first got to the dorms, my roommate was already set up in our room. Guy looks up at me and goes ' 'Sup, homie? Name's Amir Tsarfati. Call me A.T.' "

The impression Jared does makes Justyce laugh. A.T. was his 25 chem lab partner this past semester.

"Anyway, he's got some music on, and I kid you not, Justyce, the guy's playlist went from Deuce Diggs to Carrie Underwood."

"For *real*?"

---

1 headstone: piece of stone that marks one end of the grave and usu. has the name, date and inscription written on it **2** best man: best friend who helps the bridegroom at his wedding

"Yeah, bro. I thought to myself, 'Manny would *love* this guy.'" He sighs again. "It's just hard. My grandma died when I was a kid, and my mom told me, 'She lives on inside of everyone who loved her.' Prolly sounds stupid, but I really want that to be true about Manny. It's why I come here every time I'm home. He was my first real friend. I thought we'd grow old together and shit, you know?" ⁵

Jus doesn't respond. There's nothing to say.

For a few minutes they stand in silence. Then: "It's good to see you, man," Jared says.

"You too, dawg." And Jus really means it. ¹⁰

"Is it weird that we don't see each other at school more?" Jus shrugs. "It is a pretty big place."

"That's true. How do you think you did in Marroni's class?"

"I did all right. Probably A-minus at the worst."

"Figures[1]." Jared looks at Jus and grins. ¹⁵

Which makes Jus smile. Just a little.

"So . . ." Jus clears his throat. "Did you pick a major yet?"

"I did," Jared says. "I decided I wanna go into civil rights law instead of business—"

"You did?" ²⁰

"Yeah. My dad just about shit[2] himself when I told him. Anyway, I took an Intro to African American Studies course, and it really blew[3] me away, dude. I'm thinking about minoring in it."

"Damn. That's pretty dope[4]," Jus says. "So you're liking Yale over-all, then?" ²⁵

"Loving it. How 'bout you, man? You enjoying it so far?"

"For the most part. My roommate's kind of an asshole, but you can't win 'em all, I guess."

"Carothers, right?"

"That's him." ³⁰

---

1 figure (v): expect to be the case **2** shit yourself (infml): being very frightened
3 blow sb. away (infml): impress sb. very much **4** dope (sl): very good

Jared nods. "He was in my calc class. I've heard some things. Your suitemates[1] are cool, though?"

"Yeah. They're great. Prolly wouldn't survive without those fools."

Jared laughs. "That's awesome. Mine are cool too."

5   "Glad to hear it."

"So how's SJ?"

Jus can't help but smile now. "She's great, man. Loving New York."

"You two still going strong[2]?"

"Oh yeah. That girl is gonna have my babies one day, dawg."

10   Jared laughs even harder. "Awesome."

"Don't tell her I said that. I'd never hear the end of it."

"My lips are sealed."

"You got a girl up there yet?"

"Nah, bro. Lotta fish in that Ivy sea. Can't limit myself." Jus snorts.

15   "You sound like Manny."

"Pffft. I wish. That dude was a titan[3] with the ladies."

"He really was."

They settle into a comfortable silence, both staring at the head-stone. A cool wind blows around them, and it's like Jus can feel the
20 eJR on his watchband[4] pressing into the skin of his once-swollen wrist.

"We should chill sometime," Jus says. "You could come with me to New York one weekend or somethin'."

There's a beat and then: "I'd really like that, Justyce." Jared turns
25 to Jus and smiles.

Jus reads the words on Manny's headstone: *I will see you again, and your hearts will rejoice.* "Me too, Jared," he says. "Me too."

---

1 suitemates: room mates in the college dormitory **2** going strong (infml): continue to be successful, healthy and happy **3** titan ['taɪtn]: person who is a champion **4** watchband: strap that attaches a watch to your wrist

ACKNOWLEDGMENTS

It goes without saying that a lot of time and effort and energy went into this project. My list of thanks to those most directly involved:

1. God—for everything.
2. Nigel—for believing in me and taking care of the children.
3. Pop, Marcus, Jeff, Jason, Jordan, Rachel W., Tanya, Shani, Becky, Reintgen, Michael, Ange, Jay, Wesaun, Elijah, Sarah H., Brandy, Dhonielle, Brendan, Ryy—for reading and encouraging.
4. Jodi—for . . . honestly there's way too much to list, so I'm gonna go with *for YOU.*
5. Dede—for pushing and praying.
6. Jordan (again)—for keeping me on my toes.
7. Rena—for being my fairy god-agent AND my friend, and never letting me get ahead of myself. And letting me be annoying. And stubborn.
8. Elizabeth—for helping Phoebe rip me a new one.
9. Phoebe—for making me cut the thing in half and talking me down from multiple ledges. And for still loving me when I was being a jackass. (Seriously could not ask for a better editor, good lord.)
10. Mom and Dad—for making me.
11. Kiran and Milo—for being the reasons I do *any* of this.
12. Rev. Dr. Martin Luther King Jr.—for starting the fire. I hope I stoked the flames so it continues to burn.

ABOUT THE AUTHOR

© Nigel Livingstone

Nic Stone was born and raised in a suburb of Atlanta, and the only thing she loves more than an adventure is a good story about one. After graduating from Spelman College, she went on to work extensively in teen mentoring and lived in Israel for a few years before returning to the United States to write full-time. Growing up with a wide range of cultures, religions, and backgrounds, Stone strives to bring these diverse voices and stories to her work.

Dear Martin is her first novel and is loosely based on a series of true events involving the shooting deaths of unarmed African American teenagers. Shaken by the various responses to these incidents—and to the pro-justice movement that sprang up as a result—Stone began the project in an attempt to examine current affairs through the lens of Rev. Dr. Martin Luther King Jr.'s teachings.

Stone lives in Atlanta with her husband and two sons. You can find her on Twitter and Instagram at @getnicced or on her website at nicstone.info.